BEYOND THE BEECHES

Also available in this series:

Fred Archer	BENEDICT'S POOL
Peter Austen	THE COUNTRY ANTIQUE DEALER
Mary Barnard	THE DIARY OF AN OPTIMIST
Pip Beck	A WAAF IN BOMBER COMMAND
Adrian Bell	THE CHERRY TREE
Mary Sydney Burke	THE SOLDIER'S WIFE
Jennifer Davies	TALES OF THE OLD GYPSIES
Roger Hutchings	CRYSTAL PALACE VISTAS
Ken Hankins	A CHILD OF THE THIRTIES
Herbert C. Harrison	THE MILL HOUSE AND THEREABOUTS
Gregory Holyoake	THE PREFAB KID
Erma Harvey James	WITH MAGIC IN MY EYES
Joy Lakeman	THEM DAYS
Len Langrick	SNOWBALL: GO FIND YOURSELF A SCHOOL
Florence Mary McDowell	OTHER DAYS AROUND ME
Madeline MacDonald	THE LAST YEAR OF THE GANG
Angela Mack	DANCING ON THE WAVES
Brian P. Martin	TALES FROM THE COUNTRY PUB
Roger Mason	GRANNY'S VILLAGE
Cicely Mayhew	BEADS ON A STRING
Christian Miller	A CHILDHOOD IN SCOTLAND
Katharine Moore	QUEEN VICTORIA IS VERY ILL
J. C. Morten and Sheila Morten	I REMAIN, YOUR SON JACK
Pauline Neville	PEGGY
Humphrey Phelps	JUST ACROSS THE FIELDS
Angela Raby	THE FORGOTTEN SERVICE
Phyl Surman	PRIDE OF THE MORNING
Doreen Louie West	LOUIE: AN OXFORD LADY
Elizabeth West	HOVEL IN THE HILLS
Hazel Wheeler	HALF A POUND OF TUPPENNY RICE
William Woodrow	ANOTHER TIME, ANOTHER PLACE

BEYOND THE BEECHES

A Somerset Girlhood,
1900-1922

An Autobiography of
Norah Clacee

Edited and enlarged by
Diana Hargreaves

ISIS
LARGE PRINT
Oxford and Orlando

First published in Great Britain 2000
by Ex Libris *SP*

Published in Large Print 2001 by ISIS Publishing Ltd,
7 Centremead, Osney Mead, Oxford OX2 0ES
by arrangement with Diana Hargreaves

British Library Cataloguing in Publication Data
Beyond the beeches : a Somerset girlhood, 1900-1922. – Large
print ed. – (Isis reminiscence series)
1. Large type books 2. Somerset (England) – Social life
and customs – 20th century
942.3'8'082

ISBN 0-7531-9660-3 (hb)
ISBN 0-7531-9661-1 (pb)

Printed and bound by Antony Rowe, Chippenham and Reading

CONTENTS

1. A New Home 1
2. Exploring 5
3. Waiting 9
4. Lessons 13
5. Measles 19
6. School 23
7. The Newcomer 29
8. A Surprise 34
9. The Inspector 39
10. Christmas 43
11. The Sewing Class 48
12. The Summer School Treat 54
13. Harvest Home 63
14. My Grandfather 68
15. A Son of the Village 74
16. Boys 79
17. The Hurdle Makers 84
18. The Postman 89
19. Cheesemaking 94
20. The Motor-Car 99
21. The Rector 104
22. The Auction 110
23. The Rebel 115
24. A New Opportunity 122
25. The New School 128
26. Saffron 137

27. A Hard Winter 141
28. An Experiment 149
29. The Sundew 155
30. The Stone-Cracker 161
31. The Dentist 165
32. The End of an Era 172
33. Troubles Old and New 180
34. College 188
35. The Learner 195
36. The Demands of War 202
37. Heavy Hearts 210
38. The Monument 217
39. Christmas 1917 224
40. Turning Point 228
41. The Aftermath 233
42. Summer Sun 239

CHAPTER
ONE

A New Home

The first moment that I recall was at the age of three. My father would sometimes carry my baby brother into the garden and lead me with his free hand as far as the stream, where we would stand on a flat stone bridge and peer at the upside-down world below. It was with a glow of happiness that I one day picked some big red and pink daisies and threw them on this shifting mirror on one side of the bridge and watched them slide away on the other side.

This took place in Wanstrow Village, where I was born. It lay among the lower slopes of the Mendips, almost totally enclosed as a true combe should be. The only opening was a blue-stone road leading to the small railway station. All other ways out were steep and rough and made the inhabitants as sure-footed as the local goats. Our cottage was at the bottom of the combe.

Soon after that, I recall, a door slammed on my left arm which resulted in what my mother called a "green-stick fracture". I was choked with distress at the slamming of the door but my mother's friend, Pauline Warburton, gave her a tall shiny transparent vessel (probably made from split-horn) filled with an ointment called "spikenard" whose perfume was superb. This was to be used, with the bandage, on my arm. I do not know if it cured me but the beauty of the bottle remained in my mind and well made up for the pain.

We did not stay long down in the village and in the summer of 1900 we moved up onto one of the many nearby Mendip hills to a stone-built house and compound with a two-hundred acre wood beyond it. In here, it was said by villagers that a ghostly pack of hounds used to gallop on the night of Hallowe'en from one side of the wood to the other. This hill site was not far from Longleat, and on the day after a storm the sky would clear and to the north one could see the chalky gleam of Roundaway Down and Westbury White Horse. To the south one could just pick out Glastonbury Tor.

On the day that we moved with all our household goods my father was away somewhere, but my grandfather who lived with us had already arrived with the cattle, helped by various relations. This place was to be our new home! Its name was Batcombe Lodge.

"Come on in!" cried Grandpa as my Uncle led the pony and trap away to the stable, and my mother, with baby Maurice, and I stepped inside. Some food was on the two-plank table in the low beamed kitchen, a white loaf, butter, milk and sugar, while on the hob steamed a brown pot of tea. Maurice was soon asleep on my mother's lap and I sat on a wooden trestle with a little mug of milk, while she and Uncle Frank talked and exclaimed around Grandfather's make-shift table. I could see a row of pewter mugs on the kitchen shelf in descending sizes and a big clock ticked on the wall.

Grandpa's dog pushed his nose into my lap and we soon became friends which pleased me greatly.

After tea we were taken to our new bedroom, up a winding wooden staircase. It was long and low and the windows were close to the floor and set deep in the wall. Looking out I could see trees waving against the sky as I ran across the floor. Inside the sun gleamed on the bare wooden floorboards illuminating a niche in the wall. "You can sleep there" I said to Lucy, my wax-doll who accompanied me everywhere. Lucy had no nose because I had inadvertently left her out in the sunshine and her face had melted, but I loved her just the same. I pictured our games-to-come in this palatial apartment and did not worry that the floor sloped and the ceiling sagged. We proceeded through what seemed endless passages, rooms and stairs, all rather dark in spite of the sun, but full of the most exciting possibilities after our small cottage in Wanstrow. I wondered if there were ghosts behind a certain long pink curtain and kept close to my mother's skirts.

In a few weeks we knew our way round and I began to venture outside. As my uncle fetched our furniture with the heavy horse and waggon, I ran in and out and Maurice toddled behind me. Our mother settled the hens and persuaded the ducks to explore their new pond. Two of the ducks flew back to Wanstrow and we never saw them again but the rest stayed and eventually laid some eggs which mother skilfully persuaded her broody hens to hatch. They were shut into one of the outhouses to protect them from the foxes which came stealing out of the nearby woods. We could hear them at night calling to each other in the ghoulish howl that vixens make and I dived under the bedclothes to blot out the sound. I felt cosy and safe in my new raftered bedroom.

Batcombe Lodge had once been a fine old sporting-lodge but it had been disused for so long it was practically derelict. When my father arrived he and my mother worked hard to restore it and my father added some sheds. "If we want cows they'll need a stall for milking," he said, and I looked forward to the calves this would bring in the spring. We soon settled down and enjoyed the freedom and space of our new home. As we grew older my little brother and I loved looking into mysterious cupboards and corners. Once behind the pink curtain we found an old wooden box with wheels and this we sat in and pushed each other round until we could fly round the passages by using our feet alone. Maurice was quite strong and adventurous by this time.

The old farmhouse was surrounded by a plantation of beech trees which extended down the hillside to break the force of the east-wind which seemed to blow half the year round. On a winter's night it would roar through the trees outside the high wall and the house itself seemed to rock. Yet inside, where the walls were two feet thick and with the long shutters closed we were warm and comfortable before the crackling log fire. In summer the place was shady and mellow and the air was clear and good. It was enough for us children to know that we were safe with our parents and the animals, as spring brought sunshine and the first snowdrops to our door.

CHAPTER
TWO

Exploring

One day, Maurice and I, finding ourselves on our own, decided to explore the out-houses. The house had been a hunting-lodge for the foxhounds and several relics still remained among the bramble bushes and nettles. There was a magnificent kennel with its bars and its brick floor intact, flanked by a stone feeding-trough about ten feet long and a brick room behind where we supposed the hounds once slept at night. We tried to walk along the edge of the feeding trough without falling off. Then we climbed into the kennel and peered through the bars. I pretended I was a prisoner jailed from the world.

Suddenly, in a wall beyond the kennel, we noticed a door. We ran round. A high stone wall surrounded the back of the house and to enter one opened a heavy gothic door leading to the back courtyard. We pushed and it opened. We had to hold onto this door with all our might because a blustery wind was blowing but once inside all was calm and quiet. In the courtyard were several paths of blue-grey cobble-stones leading to some out-houses. One of these had a half-open door and was screened by a flowering magnolia tree. It was an earth-closet and we pushed inside to have a look. There was a wooden seat.

When we raised a small lever we found it released a shower of earth mixed with ashes saved from the kitchen range and placed in a special contraption behind the wooden seat. It was a delightful game to push the lever and watch the shower descend. We took it in turns and we did not notice that it was spattering our clothes with mud and coal dust.

We played at this for some time until a distant circular structure, half-covered in convolvulus, caught our attention. There was a wooden bucket and a pulley above it. It was a well! It was covered with thick oak planks but we found we could move one of these and we peered down inside. I knew we were not allowed to go near wells but it was amusing to see our reflections in the water far below as the sun shone brightly over our heads. Maurice picked up a stone and dropped it in. There was a pause and then an exciting "plop" as the stone hit the surface of the water. He fetched a larger stone and this made an even louder splash. He laughed delightedly.

"Be careful" I said, feeling momentarily responsible.

But he was already looking for more ammunition. Soon we were both pelting the surface with stones, sticks and anything we could find in the surrounding rubble to make an impact. The well echoed pleasantly when anything hit the curved sides. This game might have continued even more exuberantly had it not been for our dog. He had followed behind us silently but now, seeing the sticks and stones, he set up an excited bark. My mother must have heard it from the garden for she suddenly appeared at the corner of the yard. A look of horror crossed her face. "Stop that at once!" she shouted and drove us angrily indoors. We were spanked and subjected to a furious tirade and, amidst our howls, warned never to go to that area again, "Or you'll both get a good beating".

Some years later my mother grew flowers on the stone roof above the well such as pansies and nasturtiums, and it looked very pretty. I also kept a white rabbit in a hutch in the same yard, dreaming that, like Alice, it might conduct me down the shaft and through the bottom of the well (for Lewis Carroll's stories had reached the bookshops of Frome and Bath). But for now the yard was locked and we played in the kitchen or on the grass outside where we could be seen and kept out of danger.

So passed our early days at Batcombe Lodge. My mother looked after the house and poultry and made visits to Batcombe. My father and grandfather herded and milked and also drove frequently back to Wanstrow where they still had affairs to see to. Because they reared cattle, they had to slaughter and skin them and they had set up a new slaughter-house near Batcombe. This meant that meat could be transferred to the towns by train. Some of it went as far as London on the "flower" train which passed near by on its way from Cornwall to the capital. Everything was performed by hand and they needed to be as skilled as butchers as they were at farming; but it doubled their work. Through the summer they and the men toiled with the horses to and fro and in the fields. In the winter they milked, ploughed or struggled through the rain and mud with the cattle, or sawed timber for new buildings, or dozed and argued by the evening fire on Sundays.

We children absorbed it all as naturally as the Mendip air — the poultry, the milking, the cattle, men, dogs and horses working together. We were part of the daily pattern and the dry stone walls, the steep hillsides and the rustling of the wind in the beeches were fundamental to our inner dreams. I had no idea, then, that I would one day need to find a wider life, beyond those beeches, nor how hard the change would be.

In the world outside a new century had begun. We would soon be having a fine new king, they said, now that the old queen had died. We had a new home and a new village to discover. Life was full of hope!

CHAPTER
THREE

Waiting

One day, when I was four, I ran down the steep Batcombe Hill at about four o'clock when I knew I would meet my father and grandfather coming home in their trap from market. Every week I went to meet them and they would give me a ride to the top of the hill, regardless of the extra weight for Olaf, our patient chestnut pony (Olaf had been sent to us by train from Wales). This day I clambered in as usual, beside my grandfather.

As I settled down on the cushioned wooden seat I became aware of a large Union Jack lying rolled up on the floor of the trap.

"What's that flag for?" I asked my father.

"Well," he replied slowly, "the King is ill and there is not going to be a Coronation after all."

No Coronation! I could not believe my ears. We had all been living for the great village party on Coronation Day since the year had begun and the old Queen had died. I had been promised a mug with beautiful colours painted on it and thought about it day and night.

"Aren't we going to have a party?" I wailed.

"No," said my father, "the King has got appendicitis."

"What's that?"

"A very bad illness," he said.

Black disappointment settled over me and it needed my mother to drag me at last from the abyss of despair.

"There might be a party," she said, "but not yet. We'll have to wait." I did not know that the whole nation waited in suspense while Edward VII underwent the first operation for appendicitis. Because Queen Victoria, his mother, had reigned so long he was already in his 60th year when called to be King. He made a slow but remarkable recovery, but for me the interminable waiting robbed the eventual party of its glory, except that I received a smallish mug, enamelled in muted gold, red and blue, and fell in love with the beautiful face of Queen Alexandra pictured beside the King.

Waiting seems the inevitable lot of all children but its effect should not be underestimated. "Just wait!" cry the parents briskly and negative feelings gather in the eager child almost too great to bear. Waiting can seem without an end to young children and very deceptive.

So it was one spring evening. I was sitting on my own in our old kitchen, playing with my scallywag dolls. There were shadowy corners everywhere owing to the gleams of light thrown by the oil lamps. It was Sunday and my mother had gone to church down in Batcombe village while my father was out on the farm. I had been waiting a long time for the sound of my mother's return. Evensong took at least an hour and longer if there was one of the curate's interminable sermons. Then there was the long walk home up the hill. I had given my quaint little dolls their tea and put them all to bed in little boxes (scallywags are small and comic creatures with smiling faces). I had even given them a church service at which I preached with my mother's cheese-making apron as my surplice, but my mother still did not come and I wondered what to do next. My eye fell on the brass weights which we used for the weighing scales. They were useful not only for cooking but for weighing the chickens which were prepared for market. I liked arranging them in ascending rows and comparing the huge two-pounder with the two-ounce, so I began to line them up.

Suddenly my ear caught a sound. It seemed to come from the wall. There it was again, a kind of Tock-tock-tock, tic-a-tock. I froze to my seat. Was it coming from the brass clock on the wall? No, it was lower down where the skirting board panelled the lower wall. It came again! Tock-tock-tock, tock-tock-tock. It was like the regular hammer-beat of an elf or even a mouse. Perhaps it would creep out at me. I shuddered with horror. What could I do, alone trapped in that eerie kitchen? There it was again! Aghast, I realised it was coming faster, cutting the unearthly silence with an explosion of tiny fiendish sounds. I clung to the table. Then my stiffened legs slowly uncurled, as, cautiously, silently, I slipped from my chair, tiptoed across the floor to the back door and raised the latch. It opened and in a rush I tumbled outside and fled into the night.

My mother was coming up the hill. "It's probably a money-spider playing games behind the wall-paper", she suggested comfortingly. I clung to her arm as we re-entered the house but there was no sound to be heard.

The normal household bustle began again and I soon forgot my fright now that the waiting was over. My father and grandfather re-appeared and I began to think I had imagined the knocking.

But the sound did come again. Nobody took much notice this time and my grandfather could not hear it at all, although he often sat by himself in the kitchen beside the warm range. It was years later that I discovered in a book the true source of those unearthly sounds. It was the Deathwatch Beetle. The Deathwatch lives in damp old woodwork as a hungry grub. When it hatches into a beetle it emerges and it makes a hammering sound by beating its head against the wood. This is an urgent mating call as it only lives for a few hours. The sound is so eerie it had long been superstitiously regarded as a sign of impending death, because people often heard it at night while sitting in silent "watch" beside a coffin. Hence the name.

Perhaps my mother had not wanted to alarm me or perhaps she really did not know what it was. The Deathwatch is genuinely a messenger of "doom", for anyone who gets it in an old timbered house is in for trouble. But that is in the long run and we were unaware then of the danger of collapsing woodwork and I do not remember that a major disaster ever occurred to the structure of the Lodge. But I never again waited in that shadowy old kitchen all alone.

CHAPTER
FOUR

Lessons

I was approaching five years old and it was decided I was nearly ready to attend school. Compulsory schooling for all, even girls, had been introduced under the new School Board system. But nobody could say that education at the end of the nineteenth century was enjoyable or imaginative. Schools were known as highly disciplined places and included not only bookwork but physical drills and stern moral teaching. Most of our mothers and fathers who had themselves been reared on "oatmeal porridge with salt" did not realise that milk and honey were also provisions of nature and they did not complain about such unappetising fare.

Writers for children remained convinced that what was good for the young *must* be unpleasant and their writings always contained a moral and usually ended on a miserable note. There was a fable in an old book of my mother's which ran: "A silly little girl once locked a cottage door to keep her sister within; but in doing this she spoiled the lock and so could not get in herself. It was at a time of bitter frost and snow and she was almost frozen to death, before a smith could be got to unlock the door. *She was like a silly frog who would have jumped into the well without thinking how he should get out again.* The same little girl pulled the string of an alarm bell, to hear how it would sound, and a great weight fell upon her head and nearly killed her. *Children should never meddle with what they do not understand.*" An aunt read this to me one day to occupy my restless attention. "Such edifying tales," as Charles Lamb had remarked, "stuffed their little heads and starved their little hearts." This edifying tale gave me nightmares, but my mother, who had read far beyond her own schooling, reassured me that this was an "old-fashioned" story and not true any more. She had noticed that new authors were appearing in the shops and parents with money and imagination searched them out. Apart from Lewis Carroll there was Mrs Molesworth's *Cuckoo Clock*, Kipling's *Just So Stories*, Mrs Horatio Ewing's *Jackanapes* and on her rare visits to town she managed to obtain some of them. Wonderful new possibilities were opening up in education but they were slow to come, especially to rural villages like ours. My mother weighed up these problems and decided I should wait. She made up her mind that she would teach me herself before the awesome day of attending Batcombe village school. It also saved me trudging two miles down to school and two miles home, up the long hill to Batcombe Lodge. So now, at four and a half, "school" took place on the big table in front of the range in the kitchen. We studied during winter evenings by the light of a green glass oil-lamp. My mother produced a slate in a wooden frame and a slate pencil and I made lines, crooks and circles in her style until the task was done. Then she would end by reading a story from *Black Beauty*, or *The Water Babies*, and I would float in my mind into magical worlds until it was time for bed.

After a while my father was asked to bring back from Frome market a special drawing slate and pencil for me. It was going to be smoother and bigger than my beginner's block. Once again our pony Olaf plodded home up the hill. I flew outside.

"Can I have my slate?" I called, breathless with anticipation. My father looked blank. He had forgotten! The same feelings of black disappointment came over me as over the lost coronation party. He would bring it the following week, he promised, but how could I be sure? The next seven days were a torture of waiting. How would I live until Wednesday? Would my father forget again? But at last it came and I drew it lovingly from the big market basket. On the new slate my mother drew a donkey and a horse eating from a haystack and I copied it again and again. A piece of damp rag wiped away mistakes. Brother Maurice, who was envious, soon found that it wiped away works of art too and he waited to pounce whenever I sat down with my mother. I was being prepared to leave him behind once I reached the age of five and he was feeling left out.

Sometimes relations came to visit us and they looked with interest at our new domain. Both my mother and my father had a great many brothers and sisters and I could not easily distinguish one aunt or uncle from another. They seemed to eat and drink a lot and grumble about the hard times. As well as grandparents at Buckland Dinham, there were also great uncles and aunts. My mother's father, Thomas Butler, I knew because he gave us a copy of Mrs Beeton's Cookery Book with wonderful pictures and I could almost read it! (A Butler relation had started a small printing business in Frome called "Butler and Tanner" and had printed the book himself.) When he visited he called me "My little maid", which embarrassed me, but I knew his kind face and liked him.

Aunt Sarah and Uncle Fred had a son called Leslie who sometimes came with them. He was about ten years older than me and very handsome and he went to Lord Weymouth's school in Salisbury as a boarder. Maurice and I loved it when he came because he played games with us. We showed him all our pets. One day he said to us teasingly, "Do you know that if you pick up a guinea-pig by its tail its eyes will fall out!" We looked at him astonished. I had a guinea-pig as well as a white rabbit and together we gazed at their furry rumps. "But it hasn't got a . . . !" I saw the joke, but Maurice remained half-credulous. Years later I heard Maurice say to a friend "If you pick up a guinea-pig by its tail its eyes will fall out" and the friend smacked his ear.

I also knew Aunt Bess, my mother's youngest sister, because she often brought us sweets. She had pretty curly hair and blue eyes and she made "naughty" jokes which I could not understand but everyone laughed. Her husband Tom was a professional tea-taster and I thought it was a pity that when he had tasted a mouthful of tea he had to spit it out. He said he would have swallowed thousands of pints otherwise. There was also Aunt Sarah who was a semi-invalid and her bearded husband Fred

Pethick. They arrived in a very smart pony and gig. Fred was a distant cousin of the left-wing Lord Pethick Lawrence and therefore suspected by the rest of being a wicked "socialist" although he never showed any signs of political interest. Aunt Bess was a staunch Tory and wrote abusive letters about the evils of the rising "left" in England to the Western Gazette, and she in particular suspected Fred's motives. "Each for all and all for me!" she mocked privately to my mother.

These family visits increased with the drier weather, consequently my precious lessons were in jeopardy. I grew impatient to learn more.

One evening, when everyone had gone home, my mother began to teach me arithmetic. I could already count, I had so often helped my mother collect eggs from the hen house outside the back door. When a hen became broody she was always given thirteen eggs to sit on — one for luck — to ensure twelve good chicks. I would peer inside the little hutch and shout "thirteen!". I had also shared her cooking days, putting my small bowl alongside her big one and beating the mixture with a little wooden spoon, and watching her use the weighing scales. However, I had no idea how to transfer this knowledge onto my slate. To my delight she got out from a drawer in the dresser a bag of beans. These were my father's seeds to be planted soon for this year's runner beans, but for the time-being their mauve and speckled bodies were ours. These were arranged in varying piles on the kitchen table, the numbers of which I had to identify. My mother then wrote the number on my slate which I had to copy. Soon I was making 2's and

17

3's and 6's and 7's all over my slate for the fun of it. At a later date we used shells collected from the sea-shore and made patterns and shapes. If she was busy she would leave me a pile of old envelopes with a number written on each into which I had to put the correct counters.

One of my favourite games was "robbers". We took it in turns to take away objects from the other while she shut her eyes. The "robbed" one then had to discover how many objects she had left. We also tried dividing up the collection and once used Maurice as a third recipient but he started pocketing all his beans and then he ran away and hid and our arithmetic lesson was halted.

Soon I could read quite well, and write and count objects up to a hundred. By now the evenings were lighter and there was much to do on the farm. Father had been attending to new calves from the earliest weeks and my mother had chickens to rear and even pheasants which my father had introduced into the woods.

Mother, Maurice and I had been invited to tea with our neighbours, the James family at Batcombe Lodge Home Farm, who had three children and we were looking forward to that. My lessons became sporadic. But there was plenty I could do for myself and I started a "school" for my dolls in my bedroom. One of my dolls I named "Ethel" because in the James family there was a girl the same age as me. I was going to meet her soon and her name was Ethel.

CHAPTER
FIVE

Measles

In the spring we had measles. How we caught it was a mystery since our nearest neighbours, the James's, lived half a mile away at Batcombe Lodge Home Farm and their children, like us, did not yet go to school. Maurice and I were in bed and becoming increasingly bored by the restrictions and the invalid food.

It had been a long hard winter and the spring came late. The creaking boughs of the beeches were an incessant background to the struggles of people and beasts against the Mendip cold and wet. The rain poured down. At last the clouds parted and the warm sun broke through and our mother hurried thankfully down to the village.

The front of our house had two large sunny rooms, facing south and decorated with marble mantelpieces and long mirrors. They had heavy powerful doors, both outer and inner, to every room, for protection and warmth against the winds. The back of the house, up wooden stairs, contained three bedrooms, each with small-paned lattice windows. To get to a special one of these upstairs rooms it was necessary to climb two more steep stairs and we rarely went there. Through the door could be seen huge stone jars, some straight, some rounded and all with carefully sealed necks. This was the Still Room. There were home-made wines in various stages of fermentation, cowslip, parsley, rhubarb, elderberry, dandelion, sloe — all plants easily found in our own hedgerows and garden.

This day, feeling better, Maurice and I crept from our room in search of entertainment. The door ahead was open and we slipped stealthily up the steps and in among the casks. The most attractive sight was some scarlet-coloured wine, left to work through the winter months and to our delight there were bloated raisins sticking out of the top of one whose cork had blown off one of the jars. I tasted the brandy-soaked fruits and they were delicious. Maurice, who usually spurned fruit, liked them too and we ate several. Then we tried some more and they were even better. Soon we were cramming them into our measles-parched mouths and filled with a guilty delight we proceeded from jar to jar. Maurice ran to fetch his medicine glass because the juice was as sweet as the raisins and soon we were tipping back the red potion in charmed gulps. We pretended it was a tea-party and filled each other's glasses. Suddenly the room began to swim, and I felt ill. Maurice too looked pale and frightened and as we staggered to the window he was sick over my slippers. I kicked them off and made for the stairs and Maurice followed, stumbling and howling. We clung to the wall and tried to grope our way back to the bedroom but the steps seemed to come up and meet me. There, as we reached the elusive door, I became aware of my mother's horrified face rearing up towards us.

"What *do* you think you're doing! Just look at all this mess! Get back to your room *at once*. Norah, this is your fault!" Retribution had begun and we were thrust abruptly back on our pillows.

After that I was put to bed in the spare room for a week, which was not at all like the back bedroom with its coloured glass windows and my slates, pencils and books piled in the embrasure. It was cold, large and unfriendly with faded sepia photographs on the walls of stiffly dressed unsmiling people. They all looked old and alien to me except that one had a dog which I liked. There was also a framed sampler, depicting a shepherd with six grey sheep, below which was written in cross-stitch "HE RESTORETH MY SOUL". If the punishment was intended to restore my soul it is doubtful whether it succeeded. The big feather bed felt hot and uncomfortable and I became more and more bored. But I was too frightened of my mother's wrath to get out of bed, so I lay and stared again and again at the objects in the room for what seemed like hour after endless hour.

One morning my eye fell on the wash-stand. There was a jug and bowl painted with roses on a marble topped slab with a matching china pail below, and a small brass can for conveying hot water from the kitchens. There was a little china soap dish to match, on a lace mat, and even china candlesticks with two yellow candles. But best of all I liked the brush and comb. These had shiny backs with a picture of butterflies, and glinted in the sun. I tried the brush which was large and made a nice fringe on my forehead. I would be a beautiful lady.

I crept out of bed and looked at my face in the mirror. All the spots had gone. My hair looked quite nice, it was long and very light golden in colour, but it was tangled. I gave it a tug with the visitor's comb but it did not do any good. So I pulled some faces in the mirror and that made me laugh. I remembered a specially funny face that my new friend Ethel James at the Home Farm had shown me and I practised it again and again. I would go and see Ethel soon. I felt better. Suddenly I heard my mother's step on the stair and I flew back into bed and lay still.

At last my mother relented and I was allowed to get up. I was given clothes and allowed to join the family downstairs. I never passed the store-room again without hurrying in case the smell of fermenting fruit wafted through the keyhole.

CHAPTER
SIX

School

At last the great day came when I would go to Batcombe School. Two older girls, whom I hardly knew at all, were put in charge of me. They were *both* called "Nelly". How eagerly I waited for them! I would have two new friends and two nurse-maids at hand to help me into school. I might even tell them my secrets!

What misery, then, when I found myself swept up into a half-running pace for two miles up hill and down, while the two Nellys chatted and laughed with each other and addressed hardly a word to me. "Hurry up, can't you," was all they said.

Worse was to follow. The Infant Room, into which I was abruptly shoved by the older girls, was full of children, some of whom I knew slightly, but most of whom were strangers. We smallest children all stood together waiting to be told what to do. At first it seemed interesting. There were three rows of long desks, in three tiers, so that some people sat, so it seemed, raised to the ceiling. Others, (like myself, as I soon found) sat in the bottom row. The room also possessed a Holy of Holies, the teacher's desk, which no infant ever touched. But my attention was not there. It was riveted on the mantelpiece over the fireplace. There in gleaming balls of red, blue and yellow was the most wonderful apparition I had ever seen. Rows of wooden beads were strung on wires and these fitted into a wooden frame with two carved feet. It was an Abacus. Such a thing was new to me and my imagination was highly excited. Unable to resist any longer, I ran to the chair which was just beneath and climbing up stretched out my hand to the shining beads. Slap! The rough hand of the teacher knocked me from my perch and a harsh voice shouted "No you don't!" Scarlet with rage and pain I jumped up and down on the floor and she slapped my hands again until I was silenced. I found myself surrounded by staring children and a towering Miss Rawlings. "We don't touch things in *this* school" she continued, marching me to the back of the line where the other new children were awaiting their first instruction.

I waited in the line ashamed, vexed and fearful until we were marched to the chairs where we were to sit. I fancied scorn in the eyes of the older children as they strode obediently and confidently by, to their seats in the higher stalls. "I want all you new children to come here to me," called Miss Rawlings. I trembled as we approached the Holy of Holies. "I am going to write out all your names," she continued "and then we shall start our lessons." Each child repeated a name and at last it came to me. "Norah Clacee" I whispered, terrified. "Ah, you are a very naughty little girl," she said sternly. "Now, go and sit down and try to behave yourself." I joined the other children trembling but relieved and picked up my slate. Was this what school meant? Had I been cheated?

For the first hour I took in nothing that was said, too numbed by my initial ordeal, but gradually I relaxed. The rest of the morning passed reasonably well and the lessons were easy thanks to my mother's early instructions. Miss Rawlings even nodded approvingly at us once or twice and at last I began to take a renewed interest in the classroom. There was a partition at the back through which we could hear the Headmaster teaching the senior pupils. Our room had a fire-place and there was a shelf of books, in rather dull and dog-eared covers but still promising new horizons. On the wall was a varnished picture of Queen Victoria, her white head-covering somewhat yellowed by the smoke from the coal fire which burned in the grate in winter.

"Now repeat after me," rapped out the voice of Miss Rawlings, and in a chorus we began "A, B, C, D, E . . ." I had never learnt by rote before but I found it very easy. We began to learn numbers and I knew those with confidence. In the afternoon we had some stories, one was about Adam and Eve and one was about a prince. I was too nervous to enjoy them but by the end of the day I began to understand the rules. If you kept very quiet and did as you were told you avoided reprimand. If you forgot or misunderstood what she said there was trouble. There were some enjoyable things, like singing hymns with the older children, and the Headmaster had talked to us and seemed a kind man. But it was with jangled feelings that I climbed the long hill home with the Nellys at the end of that first day with that first school-mistress.

I got to know Miss Rawlings better in time and learnt to keep a low profile in her presence. She wore a long brown skirt and a black apron (to protect her from the blackboard chalk) with a tight bodice buttoned down the back and emphasising her bosom. It had double sleeves, puffed and braided at the top, tight round the lower arm and wrists. Her hair was drawn back in a bun behind but curled around the front giving her an uncoordinated look. Although Miss Rawlings was quite young she was slap-happy and hard. Her vicious slap on my right hand was often repeated on others. Her eyes were green and cold and she rarely smiled.

One day, a small girl called Mary wetted her drawers, because she was too nervous to ask to leave the room. We girls wore white cotton drawers edged with lace but to keep us warm in winter we had little bloomers made of flannel on top of the drawers and it was always a struggle to get both pairs off quickly. Poor Mary tried to wait until play-time but a tell-tale trickle escaped down the leg of her chair. The sharp eye of Miss Rawlings was on her in an instant. "Get out!" she shouted, slapping her across the shoulders. Then she steered the miserable girl through the door and reappeared a few moments later with a bucket and mop. She scrubbed and banged the floor angrily while the rest of us hastily removed our transfixed gaze to our slates. "Get on with your tables" she ordered harshly.

Mary must have lived somehow through the rest of the day but I never knew how she struggled back into class or what Miss Rawlings said to her. Soon after that my mother discontinued the cloth bloomers and several of us had the pleasure of red flannel petticoats instead. With them we wore black hand-knitted woollen stockings with garters. We were very proud of the garters because they were of the new "elastic" recently advertised in the shops, instead of the tie-ups which most people wore. Mary's story may have got round the village because several girls changed to petticoats about that time.

However, these pleasures did not compensate for the rigour and oppression of Miss Rawlings. She would shout "Hands on heads!" and every child would have instantly to drop what they were doing and put both hands up high to show they were not fiddling. Then she would take us for "drill" in the playground where we marched round in step, "one-two! one-two!" or bent and stretched our arms in jerks. I feared these drill periods because I could not always understand her instructions and because it was so cold in the winter. We longed to run about or dance but this was not allowed.

In the class-room, which was pleasantly warm from the coal fire, we learnt out of fear rather than delight. Eventually, under Miss Rawling's discipline, we did know our tables, we could read and write and repeat the Scriptures, but my first term became the embodiment of many childish nightmares. Consequently I dreaded the whole affair of "going to school".

I used to linger on the long road down to Batcombe, dragging my feet, until one day one of the Nellys thrust me into a disused quarry whose exit was filled with rubbish. There were old milk cans and broken crockery mixed up with painful cuttings from thorn and gorse bushes. "Wait, wait!" I screamed. But they both ran away and left me to struggle out of the hole and run for dear life after them. "You beasts!" I shouted as I drew alongside, but they only laughed.

After that I kept up, for even more alarming than the quarry was an empty cottage further down the hill where I imagined at any time a burglar or a ghost might spring out and catch me. It had been empty for some time and the garden had grown up rank and thorny and the black window panes were draped in cobwebs. On a winter's afternoon it appeared spooky and ominous. I could not know, in my anxiety, what a significant part that cottage was about to play in the whole future of my life.

CHAPTER
SEVEN

The Newcomer

"Don't ever let me see you going near that pond" warned my father, yet once again.

"Why not?" asked my brother, Maurice, who was at school by now although he was only four. Maurice knew the answer perfectly well but he wanted to hear it once more.

"Because you might fall in and be drowned" repeated my father.

"I would only go and look, I wouldn't fall in," tried Maurice.

"But the frogs would all join hands and *pull* you in" joined in my mother as she always did, to tease him into submission.

"I would shoo them all away," boasted Maurice, half-credulous.

By now we were going to school on our own, the two Nellys, now twelve years old, having both left school and gone into service. Our parents did not know it but we regularly approached the pond, which was deep since half of it went under the wall to water the cows in the field beyond. We would advance just to the water's edge holding hands and very cautiously try to touch the water with the toes of our boots. Mine were button boots and my brother's boots had laces and the water made the leather shiny.

One day as we gazed into its depths two frogs sprang out with a loud "plop!" We leapt back and ran for our lives, pelting down the hill towards the old cottage.

"What's the matter?" said a kindly voice in the gateway. "It's *frogs*", gasped my brother, pausing to let me catch up. "What frogs?" and a surprised lady with a bright apron joined us in the road. I had heard that the cottage was now occupied and my mother had already visited her new neighbours. I was too timid to speak but the lady did not seem to mind. She said, "I will walk down the hill with you a little way, and there won't be any more frogs".

The three of us walked together and the lady talked. She said her name was Mrs Jacobs and she and her husband had come to live in the cottage so that her husband could help Mr James, our neighbour, on his farm. Soon we were telling her our own stories and about the frogs and in no time we had reached the village. There she said goodbye and we ran on to the playground warmed by the thought that we would be passing her cottage again on the way home. Even the harsh tones of Miss Rawlings did not spoil the warm glow of that encounter, and I repeated my tables, learnt my spellings and copied my Bible texts quite enthusiastically — to Miss Rawlings' surprised approval. But alas! the cottage was closed as we passed on our way home.

That evening we encountered a stony-faced mother. "What do you mean by it, going near the pond, when you were told not to!"

We hung our heads and shuffled our feet. So the story had got round. "Norah, it's your fault. How dare you go there when you were told to keep away!" My fault, my fault. It was *always* my fault! Just because I was the oldest I seemed to be blamed for everything, even when Maurice took the lead. It was a disappointing end to a promising day and I felt annoyed as well as guilty.

From that time onwards my mother escorted us past the pond as far as the cottage and every evening she came to meet us at the cottage to take us home. It was humiliating for us and a tiresome demand on her busy day. It would have become unendurable had it not been for Mrs Jacobs. Mrs Jacobs had made herself known to my mother and already they were making friends.

"Good morning, Mrs Clacee", would come a cheery voice from the cottage door, and with a sweet or an apple for Maurice and me as we continued up the hill, the two would pause to pass the time of day. "How do you like your cottage?" my mother asked her one afternoon as we strolled home past Mrs Jacobs' now colourful garden.

"Very much," said Mrs Jacobs, "only I don't care for this muddy path around the front door. I'm going to get my husband to fetch me some stones from the old quarry over there" — she nodded across the road to the gorse-covered rockface in the hillside — "and we shall pave it".

"Be careful," said my mother, "it can be dangerous. You see" she explained "that quarry is very steep. They got all the stone out of there to build the church and also a lot of the cottages in Batcombe village. They dug it out above the site of the village so that the horses could take their loads of stone downhill — and they cut very high up the rock-face. "There's a very dangerous drop."

"We'll be careful," said Mrs Jacobs, and I found myself wishing I could come and help her with the stones.

"Years ago" continued my mother "a quarryman, George Pearce, because of a broken fence went right over the edge one night, horse, cart and all. He was picked up next morning with a broken neck."

"How terrible!" Mrs Jacobs shuddered.

"They say that for years after you could see a ghostly fluttering down in the coltsfoot patch at the back of the quarry," continued mother, "a sort of pale shape in the moonlight. It would drift along like a leaf in a rainy wind and then, so they said, it turned out to be a woman's dress. She was moving with her head bent down as if she was searching for something. They said it was George's wife coming to look for her husband, as she had come that dreadful night. They had been only three months married."

"She'd gone out of her mind?" queried Mrs Jacobs.

"When the fit came on, poor thing," said mother, "she would go back to the quarry to look for him and come home weeping across the meadow — up there" she nodded her head towards our house, partly visible in the distance. "She's dead now."

We stood in silence. I was not so sure that I wanted to help with the stones any more.

Mrs Jacobs said brightly "Let me come up the hill with you. I thought I saw some wild daffodil buds yesterday and I want to see if they have come out." We continued the journey homewards, all together, picking bundles of wild flowers as we walked and forgetting the sad tale of the quarry.

CHAPTER EIGHT

A Surprise

One day as we sat in our rows, writing out our tables, a boy came into the room with a message to Miss Rawlings that the Headmaster wanted to see someone. "Norah Clacee, please, Miss." "Wants *me*?" I said, amazed, as I followed him to the senior's room. I began to feel nervous. Why would the Headmaster want to speak to me? What had I done?

Mr Fulford was seated at his desk and he held a sealed envelope in his hand. "I believe you walk home past Batcombe Lodge Farm?" he enquired kindly. "Could you take this letter for me to Mrs Jacobs at the cottage by the farm?" I certainly could! Nerves vanished. I tucked the letter carefully into my lunchbag.

As soon as school was over I grabbed Maurice and we raced up the hill and knocked importantly on Mrs Jacob's door. "We've brought a letter from the Headmaster," we both said breathlessly. "Come on in and sit down and have a drink before your mother comes" she said, taking the note. She disappeared into the kitchen and we sat by the hearth where the logs glowed and lit up the brass medallions which hung on the massive beam over the fireplace. One was shaped like a sword and we would have liked to handle it as the crockery clattered in the kitchen but we sat quietly. Smut the cat was curled luxuriously on the hearth rug.

Our mother appeared at the door and Mrs Jacobs came back into the room with the letter in her hand. "Hello," she said, "I have some news." Mother entered the room. "Miss Rawlings is leaving and I am going to come and be your teacher in her place."

Mrs Jacobs! Our teacher? It couldn't be true! We stared at our mother and she was smiling with her hand outstretched for the letter. "Yes," she assured us, "Mr Fulford has written to Mrs Jacobs to ask her to come and be your teacher."

Our hearts were bursting with joy and pride. No more Miss Rawlings! Our friend, our very own favourite neighbour to be our teacher! Weeks, months, even years of delight ahead!

We seemed to float home on air. The ensuing weeks passed in a haze of happiness and anticipation. There would be the Easter holiday to come and then . . . ! As we climbed the road home the campions were more pink and the violets in the verges were more sweet-smelling than ever before.

* * *

Eventually the wonderful day came. Our new Mrs Jacobs let us play with the abacus whenever we wished. She showed us wooden cubes, cones and triangles so that shapes and numbers had life and meaning. We loved fingering the varied shapes and bright colours, and learned to gauge sizes and quantities with delighted speed.

By now I was nearly seven and I could read easily from all the three stages of reading-books. I had read *Just So Stories*, *Sarah Crewe* and books by *Mrs Molesworth*. I was even chosen to help other children read with the aid of a coloured picture chart — and this made me feel so full of self-importance I read even more for myself, including my parents' farm manuals and the *Western Gazette*. I knew all the current market prices for milk and cheese! There were hand-work lessons, where we embroidered flowers on cards with coloured wools. The boys had to prick out the printed patterns with stilettos and the girls continued with the creation until a row of bright pictures on the mantelpiece displayed our proud efforts. Sometimes we used coloured strips of paper to make patterns and always Mrs Jacobs worked alongside us, making us feel we were all in an adventure together. It did not matter if a child did not get everything right or tidy, each of us felt valued for the efforts we had made and satisfied by the end-product, however inadequate. Nobody misbehaved, or if they did she quickly put a stop to it.

There was a big wooden globe in the upper room and she took some of us to see it. The fire smoke had somewhat darkened the brown varnish so that it was not easy to see the writing but we could pick out many parts of our great British Empire. There was India, which belonged to Britain, and Ceylon, then Canada — one of my uncles had gone to live there, I knew, and had become rich. There was Australia and New Zealand, both British, as also were Malta and Gibraltar, and a lot of West Indian Islands where Mrs Jacobs said the slaves lived. I had read *Uncle Tom's Cabin* so I knew about slaves. We had captured our slaves from Africa and Mrs Jacobs showed us pictures of the cruel ships which took the slaves to America. Best of all she showed us England and we all had to point to Somerset.

"In Somerset," she told us one day, "if you climb to the top of the Mendips, you can see both Exmoor and the Quantocks, and King Alfred's tower at Penselwood and the sea at Bridgwater. And you can pick out Sedgemoor where the last battle was fought on English soil and where the withies grow." We had a brown and white wicker basket at home which I knew had been made by the weavers at Athelney. Because it was so wet there the willows grew in profusion and men would cut myriads of slender shoots in the autumn, dry them and use their tough fibres to weave all kinds of useful furniture which they sold in the spring.

Best of all I liked to hear about Somerset's King Alfred and how he burnt the cakes at Athelney while hiding from the Danes in a peasant woman's hut. "Without King Alfred there would not be a Somerset at all," Mrs Jacobs told us, "because when he had driven out the Danes it was he who divided our land into counties or shires between the hills and rivers, like Somerset between the Frome and the Tone, and they have remained the same ever since. She made everything sound interesting even to our infant ears. "We went for a walk to see where our stream meets the river Alham," I proudly informed my mother one day.

That summer seemed the happiest of my life. Every day I would wake with the dawn chorus and often see my father and grandfather on their way to the milking sheds. The bees would already be at work on the bramble bushes outside the linhay as I let the hens out and collected the eggs. Maurice and I would eat our porridge on a corner of the kitchen table, watched hopefully by Boxer our dog. Then we would make our way down the hill, past hedges pink with honeysuckle, until we reached the school.

CHAPTER
NINE

The Inspector

One day in the autumn, Mrs Jacobs told us that we were to have a special visitor. He was called an "Inspector" and on the day he came we were to do our very best work and to behave as well as we possibly could. We felt very excited but also rather alarmed. The Rector was the most important person who ever came into our school but this Inspector sounded much more important. The day came and Maurice and I hurried to school wearing our tidiest clothes. We did not stop at any of our favourite haunts.

In school everything at first was as usual, the register was called, we said prayers and sang our hymn. But when we older children took our seats anxiously in class Mrs Jacobs promised the Inspector would come very soon. We were not to be frightened, he was just a nice man who would sit and listen to our lessons. "Show him what good work you can do!" she said encouragingly. The minutes ticked by and we were on tenterhooks. Suddenly there was a knock at the door and Mr Fulford brought in a grey-haired man and we all stood up. He said "Good morning" with a kind smile and we all sat down, quite relieved that he was not the ogre some of us had anticipated. Mrs Jacobs seemed unperturbed, even if she was inwardly anxious, and she carried on our lessons as usual. Soon we forgot the presence of the ogre at the back of the room as we became absorbed in Mrs Jacobs' customary bright instructions and the morning passed busily.

At length it was story-time. The Inspector stood up. "Mrs Jacobs, I would like to talk to the children myself" he said. He came to the front with a rolled up sheet of paper in his hand and our attention was riveted on him.

"I'm going to tell you about something I saw yesterday," he said. "I was in a town in West Somerset called Wellington. There is a family called Wellesley there who own a great deal of land. One of the Wellesley family, called Arthur, was a wonderfully brave and clever soldier and he was a General and won a great battle for us, the battle of Waterloo. I expect you have learnt about that battle?" Mrs Jacobs nodded.

"After the battle, because it was such a great victory, he was made a Duke and the title he chose was "Duke of Wellington". The people of Wellington were so pleased they put up a stone Monument — a sort of tower — on the highest hill near Wellington, to honour him. I went to the tower yesterday. It is built in the shape of a sword pointing upwards into the sky and goes up, up, into the clouds." We all gazed at the ceiling as he raised his hand.

"Around the base, meant to be like the sword's handle, are four huge guns from the battle of Waterloo. The guns are so big you can sit on them — they don't shoot any more of course! Best of all, you can go inside the Monument and you find steps going round and round all the way up to the top." He circled his hand in a spiral. "When you get to the top — after hundreds of steps — there is a window with bars. And if you look out of that window you can see all over Somerset, even to the sea on a clear day."

I was spellbound by his description. It sounded to me like the greatest wonder in the world to walk up steps inside a sword! He showed us the picture which was in his hand, and there was the stone sword rising to the sky with a door at the foot and two of the four iron guns visible at the base. How I longed to see it!

"The only problem is," he continued, "it is very dark inside and it's hard climbing steps in the dark, especially as some jackdaws have got in and made nests on some of the top ones! But there is an old man at the door and if you pay him twopence he gives you a candle and you can go up safely. That is what I did."

I determined that one day when I was grown up I would go there and see this wonder and I would pay twopence because I did not want to step on a jackdaw in the dark. I made a mental note of the name "Wellington" to tell my mother all about it when we got home. By the time the Inspector went we felt he was our friend and Mrs Jacobs seemed to be his friend too. In the afternoon she let us draw pictures of the Wellington Monument on our slates and she gave us extra playtime as a reward for all our good work in the morning. We ran round and round in spirals as if we were climbing a tower. I could not have guessed, then, how significantly my childhood dream would one day come to pass.

So the days passed, in friendship and enjoyment. Mrs Jacobs became the friend of all our family for life. As she lived so near our own house we often used to accompany her on the way home. She went at a great pace as she was tall and seemed to be in a hurry. But she never minded our prattle and diversions as we told stories, or hunted for blackberries until the cottage came in sight with our own house beyond.

CHAPTER TEN

Christmas

It was the last week of 1903 and traditional Christmas weather, icy and clear. Extra hay and corn against the cold was needed for the livestock and the milking was done by lantern light on the dark winter mornings. Although we lived far away from the village, we were never cut off from amusements of one sort or another. The climax of the joy of Christmas was "The Party Round" and the most colourful party of all was the one given by Mrs Jacobs and her husband.

Her cottage stood near the edge of a miniature precipice left by the workings of the old quarry. It was built of good Mendip stone and covered by a blue slate roof. It was merely a "two down and two up" cottage, together with added accretions of lean-to buildings for general use. In the garden there was a well covered with three oak planks, the middle one of which had to be removed in order to draw up a bucket of water with which to make tea (and lemonade). Child visitors were given solemn warnings about keeping right away from such contraptions. Rain water was collected in a couple of barrels for all other purposes and in winter it sometimes froze, but to-day she had a plentiful supply.

The living-room was spacious and contained a refectory table and a piano with real ivory keys. The fire always seemed to be warm and bright. Over the mantelpiece were two glittering brass pike-heads, emblems of the village club of many years ago and going back in history to the Somerset Pikemen during the Rising of Monmouth. Two white and yellow china dogs stood beside them. At the great Christmas party ten or twelve of us children from neighbouring houses — boys in sailor suits and girls in kid button-boots with delicately scalloped uppers — would be seated round the table. It was laden with all kinds of iced cakes, mince pies and crackers, such as we only ever saw at Christmas time. The highlight of the feast was a glorious snow-white and scarlet confection made by Messrs Huntley & Palmers and obtained from the village shop but which Mrs Jacobs had iced herself. We considered this cake to be far superior to anything our mothers could make. It had little silver balls on top which your teeth couldn't crack but there was a Father Christmas as well and plenty of marzipan on which we stuffed ourselves.

After the debris had been cleared away from the table into the adjoining kitchen, the fun and games began — Smut the cat and Flossie the collie joining in vigorously. Usually there was a programme pinned on to the velvet curtains detailing the games to be played — Blind Man's Buff, Squeak-Piggy-Squeak, Whispering Telegrams, Musical Chairs, Postman's Knock — together with forfeits to be paid and prizes to be awarded. A screen was placed in front of the door leading to the kitchen and here Mrs Jacobs' niece, Annie, a big, jolly girl of fifteen, would stand concealed ready to hang prizes for the winners onto the long fish-hook which was slung on a line over the screen. Annie had of course escaped secretly, earlier on, through the front door round to the back of the house and climbed through the window into the kitchen — for there was no back door — to take up her station behind the screen with her "fish-pool". To us it was unquestioned magic that we *always* caught a fish.

This year, during the evening, some of our parents arrived and even took part in Twirling the Trencher and Passing-the-Slipper. My mother was among them and joined in the games. Then to my delight mother was called out to play the piano. She had learnt the piano as an outside pupil at Cheltenham Ladies College with a good teacher called Miss Theobald. She had afterwards been a nanny for the Duckworth family at Orchard Leigh in Buckland Dinham and had often played for the children there. So the Christmas party livened to the rhythm of Folk songs and negro-spirituals, like Raggle-Taggle-Gypsies O and Swanee River, as we raced round the musical-chairs or passed-the-parcel. I never seemed to unwrap the parcel but my friend Ethel won the prize — a tin of humbugs, which I greatly coveted.

Meanwhile, two elderly friends of Mrs Jacobs had come in, Amelia and George, Amelia's buxom figure clad in grey serge with white collar and cuffs and a black Bertha Morisot hat, George, stout and square and wearing grey cloth spats. "Come on George!" we all shouted "come and join in". We knew his good nature and in no time he was puffing and stumbling round the

45

row of chairs. Of course when it came to the final chair he lost and that meant he had to pay a forfeit.

"What must I do?" he cried as we rushed to consult the list on the curtain.

"You've got to lie on the floor and repeat some poetry after me" announced Mrs Jacobs, to our delight.

"But I can't get down on the floor," he wailed. "I'm too big!"

"Then we'll help you" we all shrieked delightedly, and we fell on him, pushing and pulling and tickling till he was flat on his back on the rug, dishevelled but quiescent. "Now say this after me" said Mrs Jacobs:

Here I lie, three parts of a Booby
and the length of a loggerhead!

She made the poor man repeat it twice so we all joined in. Then came the task of pulling him up. That was our turn to fall over and we all shrieked and rolled in a heap until his "prize" was announced. Then we escorted George to the fish-pool for the present — a lucky bottle which was his compensation for all the torment.

At nine o'clock the party ended with us all, adults and children, pulling scorching hot raisins and slivers of Christmas pudding soaked in brandy from a big blue dish on which the brandy had been set alight. You had to be very quick or you burnt your fingers, and the boys did their best to get burnt while the girls squealed and dodged the flicking tongues of fire.

The arrival of two dog-carts, one pony trap and two or three bearers of lanterns was indignantly unwelcome to all of us children. But no doubt our hostess heaved sighs of relief as we waved and shouted our "thank yous" and "goodbyes" and set off into the frosty night.

CHAPTER
ELEVEN

The Sewing Class

The Infant School, instead of being a place of torment and misery, had become a haven of delight and achievement under Mrs Jacobs. However, the time came when we had to go into the big school. We were secretly very alarmed although we boasted to our younger brothers and sisters, "You're babies, we're not". The pain of leaving our beloved Mrs Jacobs was helped by the comforting thought that we could still go to the Infant School to eat our lunches. We took sandwiches since we lived so far away.

"Come on in," she would call cheerfully, "I'll poke up the fire and we'll all keep warm." Then she would pull up two wooden forms around the fire and about six of us would sit and eat the food our mothers had packed. Mrs Jacobs would move quietly about the room preparing her own work for the afternoon.

"What's that?" expostulated my brother Maurice one day pulling a long packet out of our bag. "It's a *banana*", I said knowingly. Bananas had only just begun to appear in city shops but my mother had specially treated us to this novelty which she had brought with some excitement from Bath. Nobody at school had ever seen one. A titter went round the group. Novelties weren't approved of in village life. "I don't want *that*", said Maurice definitely, throwing the yellow lozenge onto my lap. I hid it hastily in the lunch bag. "Nor do I" I lied, longing for the new experience but pink with shame before the mirth of our bread-and-cheese companions. Mrs Jacobs was preoccupied and the incident passed. But we knew that while she was about, all of us were safe. I could even have produced the banana in her presence but I was not going to risk it.

Our new teacher in the big school was young and pleasant. Her name was Edith and she gave us every encouragement if we were willing to work to read new stories or juggle with figures. She was about eighteen and she wore her hair tied back with a wide butterfly bow of black ribbon and she wore a black satin apron round her waist. The white muslin blouse that accompanied these wonders was a source of admiration to us girls. It carried insertions of handmade lace which later she taught some of us to make and we all wore "Edith" blouses when in the higher class at the top of the school. Edith also played the organ in the church sometimes which promoted her in our romantic estimation to angelic heights when we attended services.

She taught us juniors in one-third of the main school-room while the older girls and boys were being taught in the other two-thirds by the Headmaster Mr Fulford. We sat back to back, hearing his sonorous voice and their hushed tones at work. The rest of us dared not disobey Edith lest we were marched from our corner to the upper part of the room with forty pairs of delighted eyes to stare at us.

One day we found ourselves sitting on forms in front of an unfamiliar boxwood table containing locked drawers. It was sewing-day. All the girls were gathered at one end of the room and all the boys were separated into the upper end where they did drawing while down below we girls were learning to sew. Our new sewing teacher entered and unlocked the drawer — not Edith at all today, but a stern-faced woman, white and gaunt, with high and prominent cheek-bones and a glittering eye. "Who's that?" whispered my neighbour, Rosa. "Don't know" I hissed anxiously keeping my head well down. It was Mrs Fulford, the Headmaster's wife, and she turned us to stone.

The forbidden table was unlocked revealing cotton bags in green and blue which contained the sewing of the older girls — considered to be "little women" by nine or ten years old. We younger girls, just out of the infant room, were made to sit on forms in front of the table and were given six or seven inches of stiff white calico for us to hem. If we could make tiny stitches in white we were allowed blue or red cotton as an encouragement for the next stage. Some girls seemed to be very clever at making tiny stitches. I tried to copy them. Alas for good intentions! I knew we had to thread the needle and the only way I could do it was with my left hand and that was a disgrace. Left-handedness was not allowed in the school and I had early learnt to write with my right hand but there was no way the cotton would go through the eye with my right hand. I dared not use my left, so I asked for help.

"Now go back and start again," said Mrs Fulford severely as she handed over my needle. "And don't forget your thimble."

The thimble was too big and I could not keep it on my finger and even when I held it the needle knocked it sideways and glanced off the calico in wildly crooked directions. Panic stricken, I jabbed and screwed at the resistant strip and ah! the point was in my finger! Tears of frustration and fury, mingled with the drops of blood began to dot the cloth. I tugged and thrust and at last five or six huge dirty stitches lined the hem.

"Bring that here," barked Mrs Fulford. When she saw my efforts and my trembling hand her eyes blazed.

"Give that girl a duster to sew, or a sack!" she shouted.

There was silence in the room. Forty pairs of eyes turned in my direction. The older boys, quietly doing their drawing, looked up with grins and nudges. I stumbled back to my seat and started to unpick my wretched efforts. Edith at the back of the room soon was at my side. She knew what I was feeling and the comfort of her presence slightly healed my damaged spirits. "Try again" she said threading my needle for me, "and see if you can do smaller stitches". But it was no good, the thimble sent the needle in all directions and Mrs Fulford's scorn rained on my head.

The whole story was told with tears to my mother when we got home, interspersed with snorts and laughs from Maurice. "Well don't worry too much," said my mother "Mrs Fulford is probably tired, she has seven children as well as a Headmaster husband to look after and she suffers from ill-health herself." I learnt years afterwards that a Headmaster's salary rarely exceeded £40 per year and that to make ends meet Mr Fulford had become the local rate-collector, going round the villages and all the outlying farms during the evenings and weekends collecting dues — often only grudgingly forthcoming. Mrs Fulford worked to help support the family.

But I felt no sympathy whatever that day, only rage and indignation. Nobody seemed to care. I stormed around the house and I threw my dolls into a corner where they stuck, feet upwards. When I went with my mother to collect the eggs in the evening I dropped two of them and there was more trouble. That night I vowed I would never go to school again, and I cried myself to sleep.

In the morning life looked brighter and Edith was as calm as ever. "You took the wrong thimble," said Rosa "The yellow ones are big, you should have had a small green one," and she promised to help me next time.

I survived the next sewing-class somehow, although I was never allowed to progress to the blue or red cotton. Mrs Fulford battled on but fortunately — or sadly — she left at the end of term because she was ill. So Edith took on the sewing and I became much happier. I even began to enjoy it. She later showed me how to do all kinds of fancy work; drawn-threadwork, tatting and hairpin work, all of which I loved, and I made a special table-set for Mrs Jacobs. One day a sewing inspectress came and happened to see me cutting something. She said to Edith "That child is going to be an expert at cutting, look at the way she handles her scissors!" We had been learning to cut patterns the new German way and she had not minded I was doing it with my left hand! Edith rewarded me with two chocolates and my wounded pride was assuaged for ever.

Unfortunately we girls were never encouraged to draw or crayon like the boys. They were given drawing books, pencils and colours, compasses and rulers, and were for ever marking off and dividing lines and measuring angles. I longed to join them but as yet girls were thought of as seamstresses, not artists. I longed to draw and paint, or carve stone like the masons in the cathedral in Wells, but there seemed no possible way to begin. Would the girls never have the chance to be as artistic as the boys were allowed to be?

CHAPTER
TWELVE

The Summer School Treat

Throughout the whole of my time in the village school, there was very little talk of holidays. Apart from Christmas, there was a month in the summer, a week in October for potato-digging and ten days at Easter. But these times were merely for children, there being no such arrangement for grown-ups. Bank Holidays of just one day — a Monday — were the only recognised ones when our relatives from the surrounding towns might renew their connections with their country cousins, sometimes arriving in a hired horse and trap, sometimes walking a couple of winding hilly miles from the nearest railway station. My aunts and uncles often came on these days, with large umbrellas and baskets of goods from the town.

Once a year, however, there was the red-letter day of the School Outing for both parents and children together. It entailed either going south to Weymouth or west to Weston-super-Mare or Burnham Sands. Oh! the thrill of it! I know I said fervent prayers for fine weather as I knew that otherwise The Treat would be off. If we went to Weymouth, it meant that my father had to drive us two miles to the village to meet several other farmers who each kindly took on the job of driving half-a-dozen children, sitting in straw, scattered at the bottom of each float, a distance of five Mendip miles to a station, where the train would take us to Weymouth. At about nine o'clock in the evening, we would all arrive home again. Our parents and the horses would be exhausted, but the children, loaded with buckets, spades and flags and "gob-stoppers" of Plymouth Rock, would be as lively as ever. I had been part of this jubilant crowd the year before and could remember all the delights of Weymouth, the little boats, the gentle tide, the bathing machines, the dry sand and distant cliffs.

This particular day in June, 1905, it was decided we should all go to Weston-super-Mare and not to Weymouth. "Why is it a super mare?" asked Maurice "Have they only got horses? I want to ride a *donkey*."

"Mare is a French word", explained my mother "and it means the sea. "Super" means "on". So it's Weston-*on*-the-Sea, that's what it means. It's not about horses."

"I don't want to go to a French sea", wailed Maurice "it's got frogs in it."

"Of course it hasn't", I told him in superior tones "It's only got a French name 'cos it sounds grand, like 'blancmange' and 'portmanteau'". I had learnt these words from the books I had read and felt very clever.

"It's all English" said my mother comfortingly "and there might be a boat as well as some donkeys and there won't be any frogs." She and I were shelling peas in the kitchen as she spoke. "Oh" said Maurice, and he ran to find his money-box, remembering there would be sweets to buy and other delights.

The journey to Weston-super-Mare was by train and that meant first a journey to the station. Cranmore station was nearly four miles from our house by road, but if it was fine one could take a short cut across the fields and this shortened the journey by nearly two miles. The day dawned blessedly bright and clear: so, laden with bags, buckets and the lunch basket, Maurice, my mother and I set off across the paddock. It was very early, still only seven o'clock, to allow us time to catch the train.

As we reached the top of the first hill, our boots already wet with dew, my mother looked anxious. "I'm not sure about those cows down there" she said. "I believe that old Daisy is still out among them" and looking cautiously round she edged along the hedgerow. Daisy was a white shorthorn who had been our pet as a calf. She was very pretty and we had petted her and she was never shy of coming and nuzzling us. But once she grew up and had a calf she grew very fierce and protective. No human intimidated her and alas! we could see a white form in the field below. We drew nearer. There by the gate was Daisy and her calf.

She gazed at us balefully. Mother tried the gate nervously but Daisy was ready. She snorted and plunged through the mud and her eyes glowed red. "Why don't we go to the other gate?" said Maurice who knew his way round the farm. "It's right at the other side and we'll get round her." "All right" muttered my mother doubtfully, "she might not see us."

But Daisy did see us. As we hurried along outside the hedge to the far side, Daisy tramped and snorted inside the hedge with the calf trotting behind her. When we reached the far corner, Daisy was there, looking more aggressive than ever. "It's no good" moaned mother, "we'll have to go back. Oh dear, I hadn't expected this." We struggled back to the first gate which bordered onto a bank, but there was a ditch between the two and we had a lot of luggage. Could we surmount it? "Quick" said my mother "we must get through to the other field!" Perilously and painfully we scrambled over the ditch and up the high, thorny bank. I nearly lost my straw hat and Maurice dropped his bag but somehow we got through and slithered down. By this time it was getting very late. "Hurry" said my mother, as we began to trail behind her, "we mustn't miss the train. We must run."

At last, hot and dishevelled but triumphant, we arrived at Cranmore where all the other families were arriving, some on foot, some by horse and cart. Mrs Jacobs was there, also Ethel James, although she did not go to school because she was "delicate". Today she was in good spirits but wore a bonnet and several flannel petticoats. The train came in, belching smoke and the cheery stationmaster waved us all goodbye as we piled into the wooden carriages.

All the stations we passed through were built of local Mendip stone, hauled there by horse-tramway from the quarries. Many had pretty beds of flowers made by the stationmaster. The line itself was known as the Cheddar Valley Line but we called it the Strawberry Line. It ran from Witham to Cranmore, Shepton Mallet, Wells, Cheddar and finally Weston-super-Mare. There — as always in summer — when it got to Cheddar it stopped for half an hour in the Gorge. As we gazed at the towering rock face, brown-faced women in cotton bonnets crowded round the train windows offering basket after basket of rich shining strawberries to the travellers. Some people gave them orders for the return journey. My mother ordered a chip basket of three pounds of fruit at "sixpence a pound, m'dear!" and on the way home we would collect it. Our kitchen would soon be sweetened by the warm rich smell of jam making!

Now for the sea! As the train trundled through the steep embankments, ablaze with poppies, scabious, woodbine and quaking grass, excitement mounted. "A prize for the first person to see the sea!" called out one of the fathers. Our noses were glued to the window. But we couldn't see anything. Nobody yelled "I see it!" The tide was out! Spring tides at Weston disappear over the horizon and that father knew it. But our chagrin soon vanished as we all clambered out and raced for the sand. Our mother joined others to look for a picnic place out of the wind and children ran about, dug castles, played ball. Maurice got his promised donkey-ride and some of us older children were allowed on the Pier. You could try out all kinds of mechanical toys on the pier if you had pennies for the slot machines and most of my scanty savings soon disappeared. A small crane in a glass case could bend over and with metal claws scoop a few lurid-looking sweets from a dish which were then lowered into your slot, and when you ate them they dyed your tongue all colours.

As we entered the Pier Ethel and I had seen a notice which said "Boats here. Regular departures for Barry Island". I felt excited. I had an aunt and uncle at Barry and our pony had come from Barry Island. My mother had promised that if it was not too expensive we might do the trip. We rushed back to the beach. "Can we go on the boat to Barry?" I begged, "I've still got one and sixpence". My mother tore herself from her companions basking comfortably on deck chairs. "I'll see" she said, and we returned to the crowded Pier where the older boys and girls had chiefly gathered. At length we reached the landing-stage and there lay the boat! But against it was a notice. It said: "Paddle Boat for Barry Island. Departure High Tide, 5.00pm". "I'm afraid it's no good" said my mother "it will be too late". Oh, Weston tide! What a disappointment you are! Why do you make yourself so inaccessible! "We'll have to come back another day," said mother, "in any case it would have been a long trip", and she turned away. But I stood staring at the stationary steamer, in disbelief.

Disappointment clouded my day. I could not forget that alluring boat and Barry Island felt like the only place in the world where I wanted to be. I followed my mother back to the deck chairs wishing some miracle would happen but nothing arose. The men were mostly asleep with handkerchiefs over their heads knotted at the four corners, and the mothers chatted on although they made sympathetic cluckings in our direction.

It seemed we were not the only ones deprived of joy. Two fathers with some of the boys had decided to find the sea. They could see it shining on the horizon and they felt sure they could reach it if they walked hard and they set off cheerfully. They returned an hour later with glum faces. Their legs were coated in black slimy mud, one of the boys had fallen over and was black from head to foot to the horror of all the mothers. They had not got near the sea but had sunk deeper and deeper in the morass. "They call this Weston-super-Mud" laughed the father ruefully "Now I know why!" and he led his son away to get washed.

Lunch was the answer to everyone's woes and the whole party gathered round the baskets laden with ham sandwiches and cakes and bottles of lemonade. There was a happy air of contentment. In the middle of the game of "French" cricket which followed, our mothers called us. "It will be quite late" they said "but soon the tide will be coming in and you can paddle." Sure enough, the water in the distance was advancing fast and it was not long before it was in our excited reach. With drawers pulled well above our knees and hats pushed firmly on our heads, we paddled in the advancing flood, the little waveless sparkling in the afternoon sun. We girls usually wore long stockings so it was with special delight we plunged our feet and legs into the living water. We wriggled the sand between our toes which looked very white in the sunlight. The boys shrieked and splashed each other and parents hurriedly retreated with the baggage.

Mrs Jacobs was talking with my mother and Mrs Sage and she had her back turned to the sea. She did not notice that a wave was bearing down upon her until, "Watch out!" everyone cried and the water swirled around her boots and the hems of her skirt. She was rescued by the publican of the Queen's Arms whose son was in her infant class. He lifted her gallantly onto the dry sand and brushed her off, while everyone cheered.

"Thank you very much," she cried as she mopped her boots, "I shall call that 'carried to safety by the Queen's Arms'".

"That's what I shall tell your husband when I see him tonight" he promised, with a wink at the other fathers present.

It was time to go home. Everything was packed up and we started to move towards the station.

Soon we were back in our carriages steaming towards Cranmore. Ethel looked pink and happy as we chewed our sticks of rock. She had not been allowed to paddle like the rest of us but she had enjoyed the games and our exploring the Pier together. Her brother Charlie had been watching a photographer on the beach and he believed he had got into the picture by mistake. "He had a sort of cloth over his head and he didn't see me!" he said gleefully. Children walked up and down the carriages shouting excitedly while parents talked over the day together, full of sleepy contentment. The advertisements for "Bovril" and "Wills Goldflake" glowed above the carriage windows.

When we got home to the station our father was there with the pony and trap. It was nearly dark but the trap had its lanterns lit and Olaf well knew the roads home. Father told us that while we were away the hunt servants had called to ask if we would "walk" two of the fox-hound puppies. "What did you say?" asked mother suspiciously.

"I said we would," answered my father meekly.

CHAPTER
THIRTEEN

Harvest Home

It had been a busy summer. My father kept a few arable fields but concentrated on milk, and after the spring calves there was all the cheese-making which, apart from beef, was our main product. This took place after hay-making, and people in Batcombe worked hard. But then the corn was cut and threshed and it was time for Harvest Tea. Everyone attended this great event in the Church Farm field behind the school. My mother in her full black satin dress and black kid boots struggled down the hill with two large baskets. Carefully packed in cloths, her best tea set was on its way to the Clacee Harvest Table. Every mother of standing laid out her own tea-table to which the public were allocated by ticket and every mother strove to give the best hospitality to her guests. We children carried the cloths and cutlery, the bread and several pounds of butter. Tea, prepared in the schoolroom, was always the same — snow-white bread, made by the local baker, thickly spread with each farm's hand-made butter. This was accompanied by tea, from the finest, biggest china teapots, with plenty of sugar and milk. The climax was the cake. It was personally donated by the village baker, free of charge and handmade by himself. There were two sorts, rich plum-cake in large slabs, or light seed-cake for those who enjoyed caraway. "Ugh" said my naughty brother, spitting out his seeds under the tablecloth "It's horrible!"

Many people in the village never had butter. Bread or bread-and-dripping was their daily fare and Harvest Tea was famous for its bread and butter. As for cake, apart from Christmas, such luxuries were a rarity. Maurice and I were careless of the tea. Our attention was on other things. There were always stalls and coconut-shies with games like hoop-la and roll-a-coin and there was even a Punch and Judy, but our thoughts that year were on new lines. We had heard that there were to be Swing Boats and we could wait for nothing else until we discovered these wonders. Mr Chaffey's brass band had arrived from Bruton and everyone walked cheerfully about. The Rector, Mr Baker, was there and beautiful Mrs Ernst of Westcombe had opened the afternoon with a brief welcome Word. Now the fun had begun and we were free to look for the swing-boats.

"Good afternoon Mrs Clacee, what a beautiful tea!" cried a voice. It was Mrs Goddard and her daughter Frances. Mrs Goddard was a lot older than my mother but Frances was the same age as me and had recently come into my class at school. I did not usually speak to her because she wore queer old-fashioned clothes and spoke in a quaint precocious way. Mrs Goddard was almost old enough to be her grandmother and she dressed like a former generation.

On Harvest afternoon she was swathed and gathered in black satin and unlike the other mothers she wore a bonnet. It was also of black satin with a frilly edge interwoven with purple flowers. Frances wore long red flannelette drawers edged with lace which came right down to her calves with embroidered flounces beneath her over-long skirts. We girls half scorned her and half-feared her at school. She was very clever and had an uncanny way of knowing all the answers without even learning them. Also she was very dark-haired while all the rest of us were fair or auburn or brown. Consequently nobody talked to her at play-time unless it was to torment her. She also cried very easily, which made the teasing even more enjoyable and rewarding, and she had been known to hide the whole of play-time behind the coal-shed.

So it was with an uncomfortable sense of shame and embarrassment that I found myself confronted by this girl and her mother with no escape route under my mother's sharp eye.

"Norah and Maurice have heard about the swing-boats" said my mother, "Do you know where they are? We can't find them."

"I know" said Frances unexpectedly "Shall I show you?"

Embarrassment overruled by eagerness, we started off together through the crowds. "Coconut shies, a ha'penny a go!" called George our shopman, who was helping in this new role. Mr Fulford the Headmaster handed over his two pence and threw four wild balls. "Hard luck Mr Fulford, sir!" cried George. Mr Fulford didn't mind. He was going to sing in the evening, in his fine tenor voice, many of the popular songs which the village loved. Meanwhile he was enjoying trying the side-shows. "Missed again!" and everyone laughed. Frances led us behind the great marquee and there we found the swing-boats. At once Maurice and I got into them while Frances watched. We never thought of offering her a turn. We had been enjoying the novelty of swooping and "rocking" for some minutes when Maurice saw one of his friends and ran off to join him. Then Frances got into the swing-boats with me and we swung side by side. There was silence, and then, "It's nice" I said. "Yes" said Frances, and she began to tell me about some swings in the place where she had lived before and how a child had fallen off and broken her leg and a Jewish family had taken her to a hospital twenty miles away in their private carriage and had paid for her treatment because her family was very poor. "And this was specially kind because they were breaking their Sabbath because it was Saturday but they felt they ought to help."

In spite of my reservations I listened enthralled, Frances knew about so many things. I told her about our new puppies and she seemed interested. Then we talked about all sorts of things and went round the stalls together. By the end of the afternoon we were friends. "Where do you live?" I asked. "Over there" she said pointing to a house near the church with grey stone walls and a large garden. "My father keeps bees in those hives you can see" she added, "but they're not there now, they're up in the hills because the heather makes better honey". That was something else she knew. "Would you like to come and play tomorrow?" "Yes" I said and we went to consult my mother who was packing up her tea table. The tea festivities were nearly over and as we did not stay for the evening party we walked home.

At school Frances now became bolder. One day at playtime, two older girls were drawing pictures of nude females with protruding stomachs and whispering to us inquisitive juniors, "that's where babies come from", pointing to the navel. This seemed absolutely correct to us and we giggled, until Frances suddenly spoiled it all by saying it was nonsense and she knew about babies because her mother had told her. She then gave us an exact description of a baby's conception and birth, as correctly passed on by her elderly mother and to our open-mouthed amazement. For this the two know-alls pulled her hair and slapped her face. But this time Frances refused to dissolve into tears. I had become her friend.

CHAPTER
FOURTEEN

My Grandfather

In 1907, when I was ten, my grandfather died. He had lived with us ever since I could remember and I would miss the old white-bearded figure around the farm.

"Why do we have a funny name?" I had asked him one day as we walked through the woods to see his pheasants. "They call me 'Clase' at school instead of 'Clasey' and they can't spell 'Clacee'".

"It was probably a French name," said Grandpa, "We came from France".

"*France!* But I don't like French people" I expostulated.

"Well, when William the Conqueror came here he brought a lot of French people with him and they stayed. A family called Clacee must have settled in this part of the country to be farmers and they became our ancestors. But that was hundreds of years ago and in the end they became ordinary English people. They moved south from the Cotswolds."

There was silence while he attended to his nesting boxes and put out more food for the pheasants. Then we walked on to the second wood.

"Did you have a granny and a grandpa?" I asked him.

"Yes, I did," he replied, "My grandfather was the turn-pike keeper in Frome."

"What's a turn-pie eater?" I asked, intrigued by this phenomenon.

"Turn*pike,* not pie" he corrected me, "And he was the *keeper*, he looked after the gate and took the money."

"What money?"

"Well, turnpikes were special roads, they were smooth and hard without the pits and mud of ordinary tracks — you know how the horses have to pull and back our carts round the ruts and wet, especially in winter. The turnpikes weren't like that, they were firm and level and you could get carriages along fast without breaking your springs or an axle. But they cost a terrible lot to run, so the people who built them charged a lot of money to use them. You had to stop at the gate and pay money to pass through. So the turnpike keeper wasn't very popular." "Wasn't your grandpa popular?" I asked, knowing what happened to unpopular people at school.

"I expect he was quite a nice man" he replied, "but people never love those who make them pay a lot of money."

"Did he live by the gate?" I pictured a sunny cottage with red roses.

"My grandfather lived at Blatchbridge at the bottom of Keyford field. He leased the house from the Marquis of Bath. The second Marquis of Bath married the daughter of a turnpike keeper, but she wasn't a Clacee! All the land in those days was part of the Longleat estate. If you got the job of turnpike keeper you rented the house with it. My grandfather came from Rodden at a place called

Wallbridge, but when the turnpikes came, around a hundred years ago, he moved to Blatchbridge and became gate-keeper."

"Did he like it?" I asked.

"Yes, but not enough people used them because they didn't want to pay the money. They made a track through the woods to avoid using the gate! There was once a man called George, my grandfather told me, who was determined not to pay anything but his horse thought otherwise. The old horse wanted to get home and he had such a hard mouth that no matter how this George pulled at him, he got onto the turnpike road and galloped hell for leather towards Frome. He was soon heading straight towards the gate, with George swearing and shouting "Whoa!", and my grandfather ran out. "He's going to jump the gate!" they shouted. The gate was very high and had spikes on top and people started to run and wave their arms. The horse came full pelt, George still clinging on, but just as it got to the gate the horse stopped dead. George flew over its head and landed on top of the gate. His trousers were caught on the spikes and there he hung! He couldn't get up or down!"

We both laughed.

"He had to pay my grandfather quite a bit to get him down off the gate and catch his horse so he didn't gain anything in the end. But they got him free and my grandmother stitched up his trousers."

"Did she stitch them on or off?" I asked, intrigued by this unusual dilemma.

"I don't know," said grandfather with a hidden smile, "But he never came that way again. There's a place near Frome called Clacee's Gate where it used to be."

"Can we go and see it?" I pictured a big white gate with iron spikes.

"It's not there any more. When the railways came the turnpikes stopped because the trains were quicker and cheaper so they took the gates away."

By now we had reached a clearing where there were more nesting-boxes. The hurdle-makers had been there, by the look of the wooden chips strewn everywhere, and one of them had left an auger on the ground which they used for making holes in their stakes. My grandfather took it from me to give back to them next day. They would be found somewhere up in the woods. The pheasants being dealt with, we continued on our round.

"I went on the train and I got my face all black because I put my head out of the window and there was a lot of smoke," I volunteered, continuing the railway conversation.

"Ah, you would have got blacker from the fire they had at Eastcombe," said grandfather. "Our family moved to the farm at Lower Eastcombe when the turnpikes closed but one day there was a terrible fire and they had to leave."

"Where did they go?" I secretly wished I could have seen the fire.

"In the end we went to Wanstrow. I was only a child, but after I grew up and married I took over the Railway Inn. They had a station at Wanstrow by then so there was plenty of trade. Trains ran from Frome to Wells and stopped at Wanstrow although the station was very small."

"Why don't we still live there? I like Wanstrow."

"It was a good place to be although it was hard work and rough at times. We ran a lot of clubs from there and we looked after people as well as selling drinks. But your grandmother died and when the big brewers took over I didn't like it so much and we had a lot of other troubles. We'd also had eight children by then but since they were mostly grown up and married I gave up the Inn and went in for cattle instead. I already had quite a lot of cattle up here at Batcombe Lodge. My father taught me how to choose cattle. I moved in together with your father and mother."

We carried on home and never talked about the matter again. It was never mentioned by my parents or aunts or uncles, except Aunt Sarah in Frome who later told me the whole story. They were all more interested in the state of the market or in village affairs and none of us ever wanted to talk about past history. Life was now and all-demanding.

When my grandfather became ill life was difficult for us all. There were worried looks and much tramping up and down stairs, sometimes by candlelight, especially to keep the fire burning well in the bedroom grate. In the extremity the doctor was needed. My father had to drive the two miles to Batcombe post-office. Here he sent a telegram by wire to Evercreech to ask the doctor to come at once. In about three hours a horse was heard and the doctor arrived. But it was in vain and my struggling grandfather had gone by nightfall.

Within a week the funeral was arranged. Only men attended funerals of men (except for widows who were special). My father, uncles and cousins, in black suits, top hats, black leather gloves, polished shoes and black socks, waited for the hearse. It arrived from Wanstrow, a long canopied sprung carriage with two black plumed horses, onto which the coffin was carefully lifted by the attendant team. The hearse set off, followed by the traps and gigues of our family and the neighbours, carrying wreaths. My mother, Aunt Rosie and I and my father's other sister, Aunt Sarah, watched them go and I pictured the parson at Wanstrow, waiting in his top-hat outside the Church, with anxious look. There would be the tolling of the bell to announce their arrival. The coffin would be carried in and the door would be shut. Doors and windows in the village would also be shut, out of respect.

We turned and went into the house, where grandfather's chair stood empty beside the hearth, trying not to let our tears show. The mourners would come back later on and they would expect a good meal which we now prepared.

CHAPTER
FIFTEEN

A Son of the Village

On the Mendip side of Batcombe there is a wide piece of land on the southern edge of the common, sloping towards the sun. This is the peewits' feeding ground and here, all the year round you can hear their wild and beautiful crying like wraiths of departed spirits yearning still to be human.

Many other creatures just as wild used to live there as well, and some of the older generation who lived around in queer stone houses seemed themselves to have something of the same wild, free quality. Stanley and Elizabeth were two such people, "veritably born of the soil". Stanley was a type common to Somerset, sturdy and sinewy with a strong round face that showed the modelling of bones beneath it. He looked as if he had been hewn from the rock his father had quarried. Stanley's father had built their house. It had two small rooms with no upper-part, the roof leaked and there were hardly any windows, and no drainage, but in these rooms eight persons had lived and slept, himself and Elizabeth and their six children, now grown up and gone. Any refuse was flung onto the common and sewage conveniently filtered down into a ditch. It had no garden so Stanley had to "find" his vegetables elsewhere. He was threatened once with expulsion but as it was quit-rent land and the landlord had refrained from claiming rent for years, the house had become his own property. Most people, when they became too old to work, had to quit their houses and move, wives and all, to the Union Workhouse, a fate they dreaded. But not Stanley. He could look after himself. He knew the movements of all the birds and animals on the common, especially rabbits and hares and pigeons — and even occasional pheasants — which improved his table from time to time and Elizabeth asked no questions. He lived out of doors and knew all the Somerset folklore and all the villagers knew him and his ways.

Unfortunately Stanley was quite remote from the ordinary levels of human morality. He cared for the normal social conventions about as much as the sow-thistle in the potato-patch. He passed his whole life with one eye on the necessities of existence and the other on the Police. For he felt these guardians of society did not sympathise with the rights of all men! So, when missing property was traced to Stanley's door and restitution was not forthcoming, Stanley took a few weeks in jail. He was often thus detained, but his wife Elizabeth, kindly and quiet, never seemed ashamed of her breadwinner's eccentricities.

She lived on "nothing" at these times, like birds in a hard winter. The hungry rooks were fed somehow — and so was she. For the neighbours were kind to her and one, the village carpenter, a thrifty man and also Stanley's landlord, refused to press matters when half a load of stone from his yard was missing at the same time that Stanley had profitably disposed of two such loads in a nearby town. Said he, with a shake of his head, "'Tis hard for the poor to go hungry when a load of stones will fill he!" and next time when Stanley was unavoidably absent for a long time about a matter of a horse and cart, the old carpenter went to Elizabeth and offered to help her with the delicate courtesy that the poor show to the poor. She thanked him — but she would manage somehow, she said.

My great-uncle, Will Stone, was one of the governors of Shepton Mallet jail and he was surprised that every time Stanley was brought in he was not in the least repentant but seemed to think that the job had been worth it.

One day, from a nearby farm, a horse and cart had gone missing. The carter had only left it for a short time while he went to have his bread and cheese and a pint from the local brewhouse. The horse was docile and glad of a rest once it had delivered its load. So when the carter returned and horse and cart had gone, there was hue and cry. First they went to the blacksmith to see if the old horse had called in for some shoes — he knew his way there well enough. But the blacksmith was shoeing two hunters from the Manor, and hadn't seen him. Then they went back to the farm, several miles, in case the horse had gone off home. But he hadn't gone home and the farmer was very upset. A child in the village said she had seen a man leading a horse with an empty cart in the Evercreech direction, so they all started down that road. But it was getting dark by then and they had to turn back.

Next day the policeman was called out and they searched for miles around. Days later the horse was found in a village far beyond Evercreech. The new owner expostulated that he had paid £5 for it, with the cart, to a man who could only be described as Stanley. Stanley appeared in court "What have you to say in your defence, Stanley?" asked the magistrate, who knew him only too well. Stanley had little to say except that he needed the money since he hadn't got any. He was soon back in his old cell in the jail picking oakum with the rest of the inmates. They had to unpick old pieces of tarred rope and stuff it into sacks of "oakham", as the ensuing fluff was called, and their fingers often became raw and blistered. But it earned them food. Once again Elizabeth was destitute.

The old carpenter went to Elizabeth and offered help with his same delicate courtesy. She thanked him, but she would manage somehow, she said.

When Stanley died, his relations interred him lavishly in the churchyard which he had probably never entered since his marriage. He should have been buried on the Common close to his native elements, but that simple way of doing things had vanished before Inspectors and Boards. So they walked him to church as if he had been the leading sidesman. The "corpse's friends" gathered from far and near on the Sunday after the funeral and walked in procession into the church at the end of the first hymn so that no aspect should be missed of the gloomy dignity of the "blacks" and of their funereal faces. They sat together and remained seated throughout the service to mark their special position, waiting till the rest of the congregation dispersed before going out again. Then, all together, they processed through the Churchyard and home to a glass of port and a good roast dinner. And that was the last of Stanley.

Elizabeth had a hard time on the Common when Stanley lived but it was harder still when he died. For her nephew took her to live in his cottage which was an "up-and-down" — considered vastly superior to the old nest on the heath. Elizabeth was shut up in comfort in an ugly bedroom that looked out on to a stone yard. She became very silent — but never complained except to say: "When I lived up at the Common, I used to see the sun rise and set."

CHAPTER
SIXTEEN

Boys

At school, most of us girls rather dreaded the older boys because, as they became about ten or twelve years old, they seemed to become very rough — if not frightening: particularly so when the Headmaster had to take a day off to take the rate collections to the nearest town. The nearest railway station was three miles away, and his only means of getting there was on foot. The lunchhour was the time for a hurly-burly outside in the playground because one or more of the brightest boys would get a pig's bladder from the nearby butcher and gradually blow it up into a balloon the size of a football — and their greatest delight was to kick the wretched thing at any of the girls who dared show herself outside. So the playground was soon the complete pitch for noisy footballers only, when the Head was away.

Another red-letter day for the mischievous boys was when the travelling stallion came to the village. Somehow the farmers always seemed to whisper to one or the other of his coming. This splendid animal used to arrive on foot, in the charge of a handsome young man, also on foot, right across from the top of Mendip above the wild Blackdown Burrows, tossing his mane, snorting and at a great pace. Then there was a closing of stable doors, a trampling of feet and a whinnying of horses, and the boys would be climbing a ten-foot wall to peep. The girls remained aloof. Such crude goings-on was beneath their dignity. But the village was renowned for its good Welsh mares and foals — so necessary to the farming community around — and the boys were not going to miss this annual drama.

As to peeping, it seemed to be the besetting sin of all of us schoolchildren. The original front of the school looked out onto the church, which faced the playground. Eventually however the old playground was taken over and made into a churchyard and the new playing place was now at the back of the school which was given a new entrance. Consequently, whenever there was a burial, the windows of our nice school-room were hastily blocked up with blackboards, but leaving many squints, which encouraged the Peeping Toms unbearably. A funeral at such a time was quite an exciting event because the Head had a big part to play in any church event and was therefore absent. He could be observed through the squint-holes walking with the mourners.

Edith did her best to control her naughty class, but the funeral procession was not to be missed. To begin with, there was the tolling of Harewell, the big bell, while the guests arrived carrying wreaths. You might easily glimpse somebody's father helping to carry the departed-one into the church. Or someone would have watched the carpenter making the coffin and knew exactly how much it had cost to fit it with shiny brass handles. Then there was discussion of the widow's weeds, almost sure to have been made by one of the pupils' dressmaking mothers. She might even be able to tell you that the widow had sat up all night so as not to disturb the high set of her hair. Her black would be worn for six months, but then the village agreed she might marry again if she fancied someone (unlike our dear sad Queen of years gone by). She looked quite fetching in her black, people said, and already had her eye on someone.

The boys became adept at squeezing the blackboards apart or finding excuses to be at that end of the room. They were becoming too big for the school and needed new outlets and excitements. My brother Maurice was becoming particularly noisy and also naughty. He joined in pranks with the other boys and sometimes made my parents very angry by his rough ways.

One day our neighbour, Mr James, from the Home Farm, met my father in the road and asked him not to let Maurice and his friends pass through his fields. Someone had left a gate open and a lot of sheep and lambs had got out and been lost for several days. Although it could not be proved that Maurice was the culprit my father readily agreed. There had been a slight disagreement between him and Mr James over one or two matters and he was anxious not to make more trouble. So Maurice was warned on no account to walk through the Home Farm land again.

But Maurice thought he knew better. Besides, he wasn't afraid of Mr James. Weren't Ethel James and her brother Charlie our friends? Why shouldn't he go through his fields, especially as it was a short-cut to school to run down the fields which led to the village! So the next time he was late for school, he and a foolish friend with whom he had been playing about, slipped through Mr James' fence and ran down the fields to reach the playground just as the bell rang.

Ethel James and I were already in line with the other girls. The boys were in a parallel line and Maurice and friend joined in at the back. Suddenly a cry went up from the assembled pupils: "Look! look! There are Clacee's dogs! Listen! It's Clacee's hounds!" To my horror, racing down through Mr James' fields were our two puppies, now fully-grown and ready for the hunt. Their noses to the ground they were joyfully on the line, tracing Maurice's footsteps every inch of the way from the James's Home Farm to the school. Every now and then they gave tongue and the sheep and lambs were scattering in all directions.

Within minutes they were in the playground, waving their tails triumphantly and leaping at Maurice and the other children with little whines of delight.

"They must have got out of their pen," gasped Maurice to Mr Fulford. By now all the boys were laughing and patting the dogs who writhed and yelped with excitement at the friendly attention. "That's enough!" called Mr Fulford. "You had better take them home, Maurice, and ask your father to shut them in." I looked at Ethel. She could see exactly what had happened. Although she was my friend I knew she or her two brothers would tell Mr James the whole story. Maurice was for it!

He never turned up at school again that day. I do not know what was said to him but when I got back from school he was not to be seen. There was a large stick in the hall and he had been confined to his room. He did not appear at supper. I saw my mother go across to the James's house and miserably imagined her being greeted by raging householders, or driven from the premises in shame, with sticks and stones.

However, she returned quite calmly and went out to feed the hens as usual. Next day at school Ethel was just as friendly so I began to feel better.

As for Maurice, he was chastened for a while and paid dearly for his disobedience. But after a week or two he was back with the boys as usual battling and daring in their games. Soon afterwards the hounds in their pen were fetched by the huntsman ready to start their training with the pack.

CHAPTER
SEVENTEEN

The Hurdle-Makers

One day, in 1908, when I was eleven years old, I came across the hurdle-makers in the woods belonging to my father.

I was very keen on escaping from the house into our woods on a Saturday morning when I was free from school. One such morning the hoar frost glistened white on the decaying leaves outlining the clumps of hazel and dog-wood. My mother had given me a small sack to fill with chips which fell fresh from the hurdle-maker's axe (later they would make a magnificent blaze and fill our living-room with a pungent fragrance all their own). I came to the open space occupied by John Jefferies, assisted by Silas Cock and both from Upton Noble. Jefferies had bartered "cutting" from my father on the basis of clearing a quarter of an acre for him in exchange for some hurdles and faggots. They would coppice the hazel which would come back into use after a few years' re-growth.

The vegetation had been sorted in various ways. A stack of good faggots stood close by the inferior ones which were for our rick staddles. A lot of poles — grey ash and birch — leaned against a sturdy oak. A little giddy bonfire blazed away nearby.

"Why do you light a fire?" I asked.

"Oh ho! missy. Why now — when there be a frost, the rods be zo brittle as glass — ye can't twist em, not no fashion at all. A bit of fire do sort of melt the frosts out o' they rods and then ye can turn 'em."

He wore leather gaiters and over his right knee was a cap of leather. He did not stop working whilst talking but, putting aside a finished hurdle, he carefully chose a fresh rod, large and straight, and glanced at me to see if I was watching. At his feet was a block of wood bored by his auger with ten holes each six inches apart and into each of which he fitted a rod. Leaning against his finished hurdles were wands of hazel and withy. With these, he wreathed in and out until he reached the required height.

Now and again, as the wreathing rose, using his leather-capped knee, he would kneel with all his weight on the interwoven wands, forcing them down together. After a bit of skilful trimming with his draw-knife, the hurdle was complete.

"There," he said, "that's a hurdle. I can make a hurdle wi' any man, zo there!"

"How many will you make?" I asked.

"Up along twenty, could be thirty. I beans zo fast as I did used to be at one time, but they be guid hurdles, zo they be," and he placed the newly woven hurdle against the stack.

The fire had dwindled away by now, so seizing my sack he filled it with fresh green chips which I started to drag home across the road, scaring away a couple of squawking pheasants. There seemed to be quite a disturbance of pheasants that morning as they had been shooting in the other wood. This was the place I would come to next year for the earliest primroses, for next winter Jefferies and Cock would choose a fresh hurdling patch and this is how the undergrowth was kept clear so that new flowers flourished.

As I came down the hill towards the house, still thinking about the hurdle-makers, I had the feeling that something was wrong. I could see people hurrying to and fro and someone was leading about a strange pair of horses. "What's happening, Sam?" I asked one of the farm men who was closing the bottom gate. "'Tis Judge Brown," he replied, "they do say there's bin a terrible accidence, up thur on the road. They took him in the house but they're afeared he may be dead." And he hurried back to the stable.

I was shocked. Judge Brown lived in Bath where he supervised a big circuit. He always came to us once a year for the pheasant shooting and this year had been particularly good. My father had prepared everything for the party's arrival. Whatever could have happened?

"Quick!" said my mother as I entered the house. "I want that bag of chips. I've got to keep the fire going in the spare bedroom."

"But Judge Brown?" I gasped, hauling the bag round the stairpost. "He's very badly hurt," she said, "Your father's gone to Batcombe to telegraph to Bath. I want you to bring me some jugs of hot water and go and call Elsie at the farm to help me. Hurry!" I fled to and fro wondering what had happened and trying to peer through the bedroom door from which there were groans and whispers. Two hours later the doctor arrived from Bruton, his horse in a great sweat. He stayed a long time and looked very grim. Then more people arrived from Bath — it was dark by this time, and my mother was everywhere, preparing drinks and food and potions, while my father attended to the horses and talked to the men.

I discovered that the accident was on our hill. As Judge Brown was leaving our house with his carriage and pair, a pheasant had flown out of the hedge right under the horses' hooves and they had shied. Because it was frosty they slipped and skidded and the carriage had gone right over throwing the judge and his driver on the road. The driver was all right but Judge Brown had fallen on his head and they feared he had broken his neck. The carriage was in pieces.

Fortunately, although very badly concussed and bruised, he had only broken his collar-bone and shoulder and not his neck. The special doctor came from Bath next day and a nurse and more men servants from his household and my mother had to look after them all. She gave them tea and bread and butter and ham and lit the sitting-room fire by the arm-chairs.

They were very polite and one of them was quite friendly. He talked to me when we both had a free hour and told me about Bath — how the London people came for "country" weekends, of the new rich business men who brought the jolly Gaiety Girls to Bath and alarmed the residents! He also described the huge changes made by the new Liberal government under Mr Campbell Bannerman, the Prime Minister. He was glad there was more care for very poor people. There were some militant women called Suffragettes in London, he said, who wanted votes for women and tied themselves to railings and this idea was beginning to spread to Bath and the government did not seem able to quell them. I was interested in all this and wrote it down in a diary I was trying to keep day by day. I wondered if the Suffragettes tied themselves to the railings in Bath too. I had heard a little about it at school from the Headmaster but our Western Gazette never told us much about national events. I had heard from my aunt Kit, however, about the new "bustle" for women, which he described with a laugh. "The trouble is they can't bend down!" he said, and he smacked his backside as illustration.

Judge Brown's assistant never came again but he had made me feel I should like to get out there, into the wider world, and see for myself some of the challenges and antics of a greater society and I felt a sudden urge to escape from village-life for a while. I was glad of our conversation. Perhaps one day . . . ?

My mother's life remained burdened for many days. But she was well rewarded and at last poor Judge Brown recovered enough to be taken home by the ambulance — a padded carriage with two horses which came all the way from Bath to fetch him.

The bags of chips were no longer needed in the spare bedroom but the hurdle-makers were always at work. They moved from one "patch" to another. I could usually find them somewhere in the woods by the smoke of their fire rising blue above the trees and their voices murmuring in the distance.

CHAPTER
EIGHTEEN

The Postman

The village Postman walked each morning from Evercreech, five miles away. He wore a navy uniform and spent the mid-day in a hut where he cut hair for three pence and gave violin lessons — seven-and-six for ten lessons. He and my would-be violinist-brother gave each other up quite soon. After lunching with his sister who lived in a tiny stone cottage down in Chapel Row, the Postman would walk the mail back to the sorting office. There was also a subsidiary Postman who wore no uniform. He used to come by a footpath across fields to get to the outlying houses and farms. I could see him coming from my bedroom window — busy reading our postcards. One day Mrs Jacobs concocted a plan to deal with this outrage. I was collecting postcards of celebrated actresses such as Lily Langtry, Lily Elsie and Zena Dare and she frequently added to my collection. So — on one of these postcards, she wrote: "Can't say much, because the Postman will read it". It was an efficacious cure! Once, too, I received a picture postcard of Sarah Bernhardt from Mrs Jacobs on which she had written in the correspondence space: "To my little friend 'Dunno' from F.A.J." — a brilliant attempt to check my slovenly speech. It was equally effective!

Later, in about 1911, after much discussion, the village was linked to the telegraph by a telephone at the Post Office and a blue notice was displayed saying: "You may telephone from here". This proved to be the greatest boon to the whole village, including the outlying districts which were hitherto served by an elderly man or woman who struggled up the steep slopes with the aid of a stout ash stick, to deliver a telegram. They could easily be from one to two hours late by this system. The reward was sixpence, plus a rest and a cup of tea if one was lucky.

From very early days, even before the telegraph was installed, this Post Office and General Stores had always been much esteemed — and so was the owner, Mrs Dyer. She kept guard over the correspondence of everyone in the village. She even wrote letters for old folk who had daughters in service or sons in the colonies. But she refused to keep a Savings Bank, partly because she considered it unsafe for a lone woman and partly because there was one with a Telegraph Office three miles away whose postmaster was her friend. He told her, in private, details of all the investments made in his office by her clients and he said she need not have a separate Savings Bank since he could do everything that was required. He knew everything!

The time came when some new people came to the Manor House and they insisted that there should be a Telegraph Office and a Savings Bank in the village itself. Mrs Dyer refused. The Manor wrote again and a man came from the Head Office to talk to Mrs Dyer. It would be to her advantage, he said, and not that much extra work. But Mrs Dyer was adamant. Then the Manor withdrew its custom and patronised a neighbouring village. Mrs Dyer was troubled but she was still adamant. Opinion was divided in Batcombe.

"Why don't you keep a dog," advised her neighbour, "and then you wouldn't need to worry about thieves and robbers."

"And how would I look after a dog and take it for walks with all this work to do and an open shop as well on my hands?" was the sharp reply.

"Why don't you get an assistant!" said the publican, "there are several fellows who come in to my place who would be glad to give you a hand."

"How would I pay an assistant when it's all I can do to keep myself with the little that Post Offices bring in" she retorted. "Anyway, I wouldn't want *those* fellows!"

Head Office sent another man, quite a senior one this time. "Mrs Dyer," he said, "we are wanting to install a new Post Master here, who will manage the Telegraph and Savings Bank as well as the post, and we would like you yourself to assist him as well as look after the Stores."

"Oh would you," she said. "So I'm to be thrown out, am I?"

"Not at all," said the senior man "but we are inviting you to expand, to make the business bigger and better paid."

"Thank you, I'm quite all right as I am," she answered, "and I don't want any strange Post Masters managing my work for me, pay or not pay."

Finally Head Office sent the Manager. "Mrs Dyer," he said, "as you know, we are hoping to expand the Post

Office system and we are trying to do it by employing some of the men who left their jobs to go and fight for us. We are wondering if you could help?"

"And how would I do that?" Mrs Dyer asked suspiciously.

"Well, Mrs Dyer," he said, with a cautious glance at her, "There is a man we have in mind who has just got back to England after fighting in the Boer War and he lives in this village. He is a good business man — but unfortunately he has lost a leg. He was in the Relief of Mafeking with General Buller."

"Oh! you mean — my nephew?" said Mrs Dyer, transfixed. "Yes," said the official. "He has never mentioned it," said Mrs Dyer, surprised. The manager smiled. "I expect you know he is getting married very soon, now he is home in Batcombe?"

"He's marrying my friend Jane, down in the village," she replied with mounting excitement.

"Well, how would it be if the two of them helped with the Post Office *and* managed the Telegraph *and* a Savings Bank alongside you?" Mrs Dyer was radiant.

"Why that would be wonderful," she said. "What's more, they could live in my house. Since my husband died it has been far too big for me, and with the garden as well I have been wondering how ever I was going to manage. I was nearly overcome last winter when I had influenza. I find it hard to keep going."

"So may I offer him the job?" said the Manager.

"Of course you may," agreed Mrs Dyer, "and that, as soon as possible."

Everyone was pleased and it wasn't long before the people at the Manor returned also. Mrs Jacobs sent me a card with the new Telegraph stamp on it. She wrote "First Day Cover. Keep this stamp as a souvenir."

CHAPTER
NINETEEN

Cheesemaking

The industry to last longest in the village was Cheddar Cheese making. In school we wrote down, "The art of cheese-making was not known to the ancient Britons but was learnt from their Roman conquerors. Cheese is the curd of milk, dried until it is solid." The lactic acid, naturally present in a calf's stomach, converts the cow's milk into curd to provide the calf with food, when it drinks her milk, as we knew whose mothers made cheese.

Mr Fulford then told us in his sonorous voice "The Romans discovered that this process did not require a living calf but that any piece, taken from its stomach after its slaughter, would curdle the milk provided the weather was warm enough. This knowledge was passed on to the early Britons in Wessex, where the cow pastures were particularly rich. When Batcombe Manor was given to Glastonbury Abbey, in 940 AD, by Edmund King of Wessex, the Abbey monks encouraged cheese-making on the farms of their estates. St. Dunstan, first Abbot of Glastonbury who died a thousand years ago, would almost certainly have eaten 'Cheddar Cheese' with his bread." Mr Fulford knew all the history of Somerset.

The majority of our farms produced cheese. In Batcombe the most economically rewarding use of the land was in dairy products rather than in arable, because corn and wheat did not fetch high prices and our grass was particularly rich. So in summer after the spring calves, when there was an abundance of magnificent milk for cheese and in winter when there was still enough milk for good butter, all our efforts went into the cows. At both seasons, making full use of the milk was an essential economy but it could rarely be used in liquid form for drinking. There was no means of transporting milk to the towns and so no market for fresh milk. Townspeople mostly drank beer.

My grandfather once told me that in his day, at cheese-making time when the weather warmed up, a calf's stomach was obtained from the butcher, cut into strips and dried from the kitchen rafters. Each day when the cheese was being made a few inches were cut off and placed in the tub of milk to sour or "curd" it. By my day, in 1905, the lactic acid could be obtained from the chemist in a bottle, together with an instrument called a "lactometer" for measuring correct amounts. This was a modern invention and fortunately saved us a great deal of work. But I knew that once cheese-making began everything was bustle and nerves were frayed and I could expect no attention from my mother until it was over.

On some farms the cows were milked in the fields by the farmer and his wife, or by maids, sitting on three-legged stools; but we brought our cows into sheds. The milk for cheese was brought into the dairy in silvery pails and run over cooling water pipes and then transferred into huge tubs to which the rennet was added. These were covered with linen cloths and left till next day. Then my mother would come and break up the "junket" gently, with a long spoon, and drain off the whey through a tap at the bottom. The remaining curds tested by the lactometer were soon ready to be piled into small blocks and covered for a few more hours.

Next these were pounded and put in a spotlessly clean muslin-lined vat and the whole lot placed under a cheese press. This had to be tightly squeezed by two wooden arms to drain it once again until finally after two or three days, it was taken out, shaped ready to stand upright.

All the implements were then scalded and cleaned with boiling water from the huge copper, suspended over the ever-burning furnace and supervised by my mother.

We wrapped the cheeses in new clean cloths and they were taken away to the cheese-room to be ripened. It needed three months for a small buckle and up to six months for a one-hundred-weight cheese to ripen. Sometimes my mother sought advice from Mrs Sage at Vale Farm. Mrs Sage had won prizes at Frome Show and had excelled over competitors from all over the British Empire, and Batcombe was proud of her. Every maker had her own "touch" but all wanted to produce the very finest "Cheddar" and Mrs Sage's advice was sought throughout Somerset.

The day would come when the dealer arrived to test the cheeses. With a long-handled scoop which had a sharp-cutting edge he would take a very small piece from the centre of a giant cheese and sample it. We would watch, expectantly, to see his reactions. If he considered it "sweet and sound" he would give us as much as ten-pence ha'penny a pound for it or even a shilling in a good year. Then he and my mother's cheese-maker (she did not do all the work herself) would carry the cheeses out to the horse and waggon waiting outside. Some of the cheeses were so heavy it needed two men to lift them and the assistant cheese-maker could receive up to fourteen shillings a week for his work if he was lucky.

However, they were not all lucky. There was one wealthy cheese-farmer in an outlying district whose wife was well known for her meanness. She kept a maid to do the housework so that she herself could attend to the cheese, and she employed a cheese-maker. The maid had to sleep in a freezing attic with only a candle for light and she was allowed only whey-butter on her bread while all the rest of the family ate dairy-butter. The wife was also so suspicious that she made her husband walk continually up and down the dairy to supervise the cheese-maker. So the husband did this, at the same time keeping his hands behind his back with a big chunk of cheese wrapped in a piece of paper. This he used to slip, unbeknown to his wife, to the hungry cheese-maker to take home with him.

One day, just as he was passing over his package the wife came in. "What the devil are you doing!" she shouted, snatching the packet. "Why are you giving him cheese?" The farmer stammered " I — I — I was just . . ." With great presence of mind the employee intervened:

"Pardon me, ma'am, but your husband was keeping this piece of cheese wrapped so that I could take it to your kitchen for your table. There are a lot of tramps and vagabonds about these days and if they saw me crossing the yard with a big piece of cheese they would be sure to come and beg and we might have to give some away."

Only partly mollified the stingy wife sniffed and continued on her sharpeyed round. Next day there were *two* pieces of cheese in the package, one for the kitchen table and one for the cheese-maker's pocket. But the poor maid never got any cheese at all and she left at the end of the summer.

CHAPTER TWENTY

The Motor-Car

In 1907 it was common to travel long distances by train but as yet nobody in our village had ever ridden in a car. There were only horses on the road and no motors at all. However, we had seen one of the new "motor-waggons" on display when we went to a festival day in Frome. It had caused some excitement but most people said it was just a craze and it wouldn't last long. Some said also that it was dangerous to travel at ten miles an hour as the heart might stop beating, or your hair might fall out!

However, someone in the village had been to London and he had seen several motors there — "Like ordinary waggons," he said, "but moving under their own steam power without a horse." Then a family arrived from Bristol and they had also seen "motor-cars", as they had come to be called, and we envied them. Then one day we saw them for ourselves. We had driven in the pony and trap to Shepton Mallet, as my mother wanted to visit her Aunt Stone. Part of Shepton Mallet gaol had been burned down some weeks before and as her uncle was one of the governors of the gaol Aunt Stone had a lot to tell her about it all. Great Aunt Stone wore a frilled lace cap and had expensive furniture. Tea was served on a polished Pembroke table.

As we sat in the parlour we heard a chugging noise and through the window we saw two motor-cars passing! We jumped from the table.

Maurice and I rushed out into the garden and gazed at them through the gate. Yes, they really were waggons that ran along without a horse! They were like huge leather armchairs high up on wheels. Steam hissed out of the sides in irregular clouds. The men who sat in them looked very pleased with themselves and they held brass wheels in their hands with which they steered the chugging waggons. They wore peculiar hats and "goggles" over their eyes, and they had rugs over their knees, as we did in the trap. Maurice was delighted and could talk about nothing else all the way home. "I wish I could have a ride in one," he lamented. But I was frightened of this "monster".

After a while the number of motor-cars increased and we even saw some passing through the village. One of the sons at the Manor had one and he loved to show it off by parading down the street. They were now powered by petrol and smelt strongly. Very occasionally visitors passed right up our road in their new machines although the hill was an effort for their puffing engines. Of course it alarmed the horses and made them shy, but we were acclimatised by now.

One day, I was walking along our road when I heard a chug-chug behind me. It was a new motor-car and there was a dashing friendly-looking man behind the wheel. "Like a ride?" he called as he drew up beside me. I was overjoyed and I scrambled up beside him. He had to yank a handle in the front to make it start again but soon the engine sputtered, then chugged, and we were off. It was very exciting to be perched up high among the shiny fitments moving even faster than a horse but without a horse! I hung on very tightly and the driver laughed. When we reached our gate he stopped and helped me down. "Thank you very much," I said and rushed to our house to report my good luck.

"You shouldn't have accepted a ride," said my mother frowning "you didn't know who he was or what he might do." "But it was so nice," I expostulated, disappointed at my reception. "Nice or not," retorted my mother "you should not have got in. Don't you ever do that again," and she slammed the door.

I felt vexed and angry. My triumph was spoilt. I had been looking forward to telling them all. "Go and shut up the chickens," called my mother abruptly, "it's getting late and I don't want them out on their own when that fox is about." Usually I enjoyed shutting the tiny fluffy chicks into the coops with their mothers, but this evening I didn't feel like it at all. I felt guilty, angry and unjustly treated as I stamped out to the hen-coops.

My mother had a lot of hens, Plymouth Rockers and Rhode Island Reds in particular. As each hen went broody she was shut in a separate coop where she sat for three weeks on her eggs until the chicks hatched out and emerged. This evening I managed to get most of them back into their coops but one batch was particularly active. The little yellow fluffy babies fled to and fro while the old mother clucked and strutted. Eventually they all ran between the bars and underneath her feathery wings — except for one. This one would not go

101

in. He ran up and down and just as he was going to enter rushed out again. At last he ran in and I went to drop the slats, but out he burst again! I was exasperated. I picked up a stone and flung it at the little creature. It hit him straight on the head and he fell to the ground and lay still. When I went to pick him up, his eyes were shut. He was dead.

I was appalled. I had not meant any harm but he lay in my hand and I could not get him to move. What would I say to my mother? She was already annoyed with me and now I had done this. Really guilty now I crept down to the sheds where my father was milking.

"I've killed a chicken by mistake," I said.

"You'd better tell your mother."

"Yes," I said miserably, and trailed back to the house. I knew my mother was in a bad mood and I would probably get slapped. But it wasn't so bad after all. My mother had almost recovered her good temper. She had just got the grandfather clock to go, which had not worked for weeks. She was quite matter-of-fact about the chicken. "Go and bury it in the garden," she said "and then call everyone in for tea."

It was beginning to grow dark as I found a spade and dug the hole. The baby chick was lying where I had left it and the rest had settled for the night under their mother's wings although I had not dropped the overnight slats. Shutting the coop I said "Sorry" to the anxious mother hen and I took the limp handful of fluff to the garden. We had buried chickens before but I hated seeing the black soil mar the pretty yellow down on its head and chest. I put a stick over the place to look like a cross to complete the solitary funeral.

As we sat over tea in the kitchen my parents talked to Uncle Fred, who had recently come to stay since my Aunt Sarah had died and Leslie had gone away to college. Nobody mentioned the motor-car and it never came our way again. But when I told Maurice about it he was filled with envy and went down to the village to see if he could find a ride for himself. When motors eventually came up our hill they were mostly trades-vans and not nearly as polished and magnificent as that first automobile.

CHAPTER
TWENTY-ONE

The Rector

Churchgoing for us was not an easy matter. After walking two miles to school each day and two miles back we wanted a rest at weekends. My father rarely attended the church, having numerous jobs to attend to on the farm, so it meant walking with my mother. The service was usually Matins and took two hours. We children entertained ourselves by trying to read the wall plaques or noting the antics of the choir boys or the hats worn by the ladies from the Rectory. Once the service had begun there was the puzzle of finding the place in a prayer book with Latin headings. I was privately mystified by the words and chants we were invited to join in but supposed that being "spiritual" must be equal to being incomprehensible. After swearing we were miserable sinners, chanting Venite, Te Deum and Benedictus, there were two long readings by the Rector. Then there was the sermon to endure, enlivened finally by the sidesmen with brass collecting plates. We knew these men well on week days in their working clothes but only just recognised them in their stiff shiny Sunday suits and collars, with hair damped down and their boots highly polished.

The Rector was a powerful character with two sons and several daughters. He ran the Church on Sundays as he ran his family on week-days, with arrogance and splendour. He was considered a fine horseman and kept a carriage and wore a top hat. Batcombe Rectory was a mansion and in the past he had founded a school in its grounds. This was for about thirty young men, many of whom had been expelled from their public schools but whose parents wanted them to study for the new entrance examinations for the Army. The tutors lodged in various big houses in the village and the pupils in the Rectory. Wooden huts were erected in the grounds as dining-room, billiard room and classrooms. This crowd brightened the village and the public-houses considerably — with disastrous results. It had unfortunately brought discredit to several families in the village and by 1894 the Rector had gone bankrupt and had to sell up his coaching establishment and move away, leaving all the administration to a curate.

He continued however to be Rector of the Parish and returned after a while in even greater splendour. One day he was driving along with his carriage and pair when he met my youthful uncle Frank with his horse and cart. My uncle refused to pull in sufficiently far to the side of the road to make room for the oncoming carriage to pass. Whereupon the Rector slashed Uncle Frank across the face with his horsewhip, "to teach the young puppy a lesson" — a lesson which Frank, who was only eighteen, never forgot or forgave. He swore he would have his revenge one day and whenever he could he caused trouble to the Rectory household from that day onwards.

The Rector was a keen hunting man and he rode to hounds twice a week. At meets he would ride up to the Master and tell him where foxes had recently been seen — including the vixen and her cubs which inhabited our woods. Then he would canter off and take his stance beyond the trees on his great black hunter. He was the first to holler when the fox broke cover and away he would gallop behind the huntsman, followed by the field, with the horn doubling "Gone away!" and the fox flying for its life.

At a lawn meet he would toss off several glasses of whisky served from the big house, and touch his top-hat with a courteous sweep of his crop to the skirted ladies on their side-saddles, or he would flick his lash at a stray hound all of whose names he knew — Dimity, Dainty, Ransome or Roister. His horses were hogged and docked which scandalised me who had recently read "Black Beauty". They were well fed however and smartly turned out by the village lads who were his stable-boys. The men also had orders to set up fences around his land which extended as far as our woods.

The enmity between the Rector and my hot-headed uncle grew and one day it reached crisis point.

The Rector loved shooting and invited large parties to the Manor in the pheasant season for a shoot. It happened that he also owned a 25 acre wood, adjoining the woodland owned by my father. In those days of 1905, shooting pheasants was a regular country occupation and Frank was particularly interested in breeding a special variety of pheasant called Golden Eye. He and the keeper were very successful in rearing a number of these delicate chicks into fine fully-plumed birds which thrived within our woodland. In spite of the prowling foxes, until our own autumn shoots began, Frank nursed the young birds to maturity.

Meanwhile the Rector, seemingly to outdo us with his pheasants, set up a rick of wheat-stacks in his wood, right close to the hedge which divided the two properties. This gave his pheasants a plentiful supply of grain and straw to eat and to scratch in. Unfortunately it lured our pheasants away from their original home to the other side of the fence where the grain was plentiful. So when the next shoot arrived at the great house, Uncle Frank saw some of his favourite Golden Eyes disappearing into the Rectory bags. He was furious.

One night, unable to bear it any more, he slipped through the wood to the rick. Silently he put a lighted match to the straw. It blazed high above the fence. Soon there was nothing left of the rick but a dusty mass of blackened reed.

It wasn't long before a man in navy blue uniform appeared at our house as Maurice and I were one day making something with Uncle Frank in the garden. The policeman and Frank walked off together leaving us to carry the exciting news indoors to our parents. Uncle Frank was given fourteen days detention and required to pay costs. Most people felt the plaintiff should have been given the same punishment but my uncle paid dear for his misdeeds. When Frank attained his majority he went away to London and joined a Jewish business firm and did exceedingly well, but he died young.

As local children we were supposed to curtsey to the Rector's daughters but our fathers forbade us to do so. One day a friend called Rosa and I were walking along a lane which led down to the village. All of a sudden we heard horse's hooves behind us and on turning round we saw the governess-cart approaching from the Rectory. One of the Rector's daughters was driving and another was inside it with some children. We stepped in close to the bank. "Don't curtsey" hissed Rosa urgently, as she pressed against the long grass. "No, I won't" I muttered and we stood staring fixedly ahead of us. The cart stopped and the driver leant towards us. "Got stiff knees this morning?" she asked in sarcastic tones. With our legs obstinately straight we made no reply but walked on. The children stared at us from underneath their frilly bonnets. "What manners!" exclaimed the Rector's daughter as she swung her whip and continued with her precious load down the hill.

The Rector was Squire to the village as well as being its parson and most people stood in awe of him. However, when my grandfather was dying the Rector visited him several times, which was generous considering my grandfather had rarely been near the church. Finally the Rector himself had a stroke and died and there was a long interregnum.

In the school a coloured clergyman was brought in from the chapel in the village. He was a Wesleyan, who taught us well, but he and his English wife soon went away again to the missionary work they had left before. Then followed a curate who did not last long either because he was epileptic. Mrs Jacobs would rush from the Infant Room and put a rolled-up coat under his head when he fell in one of his fits. In his teaching he insisted that there was no such thing as Hell Fire but only a Black Hole. On consideration, I reckoned I preferred the former — it would be more in keeping with Joan of Arc whom I admired from history books.

During all these changes, the church and village were waiting for the appointment of a new Headmaster as well as a new Rector, for Mr Fulford was leaving.

CHAPTER
TWENTY-TWO

The Auction

Mr Fulford, our Headmaster and family friend of so many years, had retired, overstrained by the work of the school and the care of his ill wife and peculiar youngest son, Edward. What was even worse was that our beloved Mrs Jacobs announced, to our dismay, that she and her husband had decided to emigrate to Canada. The fever of emigrating west was gathering momentum and several of Mr Fulford's sons had already gone to Canada. Life seemed all change. It was hard to adjust to the loss.

We now had no older friend to accompany us on the winding road to school and no Headmaster to greet us on arrival.

One day a letter arrived from Mr Whittuck, the solicitor. When my mother read it she hurried out to fetch my father and they both sat at the table looking shocked.

"Mr Whittuck says he has instructions to sell Batcombe Lodge," my mother explained later. "Doesn't it belong to us?" I asked, amazed. "No, it belongs to a family called Bailey Neale over at Nunney and we only rent it. Now Squire Bailey Neale has died and they have ordered the solicitor to sell the whole estate." "What is going to happen?" I begged. "It is to be put up for auction next month in Frome. We can buy it if we like but we have to bid for it on the open market." We were all very upset. What should we do? "Whatever happens you must buy it," said my mother to my father, "even if it leaves us in debt."

"I'll come with you for support," said my Uncle Fred who by that time had come to live with us. He was rather tiresome, always present in our affairs but we were sorry for him being a widower, now that Aunt Sarah had died.

A month later the two set off for Frome and we wished them luck and then set about the day's work, on tenterhooks for their return. My parents had more or less agreed on a ceiling price but it included possible variations. The day dragged on and we could not concentrate on anything. I re-arranged my bedroom to make the time pass.

When at last my father's trap was heard returning my mother ran out. "Did you get it?" she called eagerly. "No," replied my father. "I was outbid." He dismounted slowly and went to the pony's head. "Do you mean you've let Batcombe Lodge be sold to someone else!" gasped my mother.

"Yes," he said. "Who to?" "To our neighbour," said my father. "Mr James?" cried my mother, incredulously. "Yes," he said.

We felt stunned. We had never dreamt that Mr James was even thinking of it. Did that mean that Ethel would move into my home and we have to go away? The thought was unimaginable. Why hadn't they mentioned it?

"Well," explained my father, "it came to the top price and I didn't want to bid against my neighbour and Fred here, he said 'Wait'." Uncle Fred looked uncomfortable and attended to the pony.

"I would have said 'Go on'!" expostulated mother, "Why didn't you?"

"Ah — but you see," he continued, "they were also selling Batcombe Woods as a separate lot, and we were offered 200 acres of land, buildings, woods and all, at a far better price than we would have paid for the Lodge land which is small. So I bought it."

"Bought it?"

"Yes, I bought Batcombe Woods."

"But there isn't a house! We can't sleep in a wood! What are we to do?" cried mother again "How do we get a house?" "Build one," said father, "we must build our own house."

And that is what we did.

It was a daunting task. There were two woods, large and small, with a small paddock in the middle. First the men set about clearing five acres of hardwoods, leaving the larger oaks and beeches as protection against the Mendip winds. The trees had to be sawn by hand and the roots grubbed up one by one by toiling men and horses. They all but broke under the strain but somehow it made progress. When it was achieved a herd of goats was then brought in to demolish any new sproutings. Finally the whole plot was ploughed up and sewn with grass, but that took several years to grow.

Before the new house could be planned at all we had to find water. Across the road at Batcombe Lodge we had always used rain water from an underground tank or drinking water (which was always boiled) from the spring in the field which never dried up. Now we had to find it and the hills in the Mendips are often topped with so deep a layer of limestone it is hard to reach water. My father therefore employed a dowser who lived in the neighbouring village of Horningsham about seven miles away. He had to be fetched and returned and he charged seven shillings and sixpence plus a free lunch to come and divine our water, but my father felt it was worth the enormous cost.

First the dowser went to the hedge and cut a V-shaped hazel twig. Then he tramped briskly around the young oak-tree area where my father hoped for a well. Nothing happened and we who were watching felt quite disappointed. "Watch the stick in his hand," said my father. All of a sudden the twig began to twist itself over and over and quiver and kick. He had come to the hidden course of the stream some fifty feet below the limestone and it was telling him this as if it were a living thing.

"There you are," he said, "now you can start to dig."

Sure enough, when the men dug down the water spouted up. A new-style artesian well was sunk, and an oil-driven engine and pump installed and this well never failed. Meanwhile an architect had been found in Salisbury to design our new home and a builder from Frome supplied the special red bricks — not porous grey Bath stone like Batcombe Lodge across the road. The bricks arrived on a cart but the tools came on a real motor-waggon which we all ran out to admire. I was becoming quite excited by this time. I had heard that

113

there was to be a real up-to-date flush lavatory in the new house and taps for water. Best of all there would be a bath-room with a special bath, which my mother had seen advertised, made of imitation polished marble in mottled pink and grey.

The great day came and all our furniture was moved over from the outbuildings to "The Beeches" as the new house was called. The James family had already moved into the Lodge and left their farm which was a beautiful ancient house with its own chapel but it was remote from other people and down a long lane. Mrs James was unwell and she did not like the lonely situation so she had persuaded Mr James to make a bid for Batcombe Lodge when it came up for sale so that they would be nearer the road. It created considerable tension between our two families. Ethel and I remained friendly in spite of the adults' bitterness, but we met at school rather than in our houses.

Had we gained or lost? We never knew. Men and horses had struggled and toiled to their limit, the hillsides were so steep it was excessively gruelling for the horses. Every inch of the land had to be won back from the woodland before it could be cultivated. My parents were perpetually worried and exhausted, and they were desperately hard up because no money came in all that time. But eventually a real farm was created and our very own homestead established among the beech trees.

CHAPTER
TWENTY-THREE

The Rebel

Although kind old Mr Fulford had retired from the school he remained in the village and we saw him at church, often with his youngest son Edward. Edward was starting training as a clockmaker and doing well but he still had "queer turns" as people said in the village.

The new Headmaster had arrived and he was dynamic. His name was Mr Stenning. Our learning took on a new dimension under him. I was eleven and so was Frances and we were in the top school. We began to experience a new delight in music and poetry. Mr Stenning introduced our class to Shakespeare and we acted scenes from *A Midsummer Night's Dream* and *The Merchant of Venice*. He also taught us science, explained the attempts to split the atom and how they found the new oil-fields in Scotland. He took us to the old quarry which revealed, not merely the old dangers, but beautiful ammonites that we had never dreamt existed there and we studied the geology of our area. One night he took us older ones to see Halley's comet which was due that year. We were very excited to be out so late. We had to look through blackened glass in order not to hurt our eyes by the comet's bright light. We did this adventure for about a week and felt very superior as astrologers.

Frances and I admitted to each other secretly that we didn't see anything except a shadow but we pretended we did.

The boys were now taught woodwork and gardening, while we girls, to our delight, were taken to Evercreech to learn cookery (except those whose mothers considered this their own prerogative and kept their daughters at home). We rode in a pony and trap, with a huge green umbrella if it rained, provided by Mr Gibbons our driver. The teacher, Miss Hebditch, was trained by the county, and she provided us with white sleeveless pinafores. (The class was a new venture by the Government). We cooked in coke-heated ovens and produced relays of potato soups, cottage pies, cakes and tarts, which our families unfortunately gobbled so fast we became committed to cooking them regularly. Sometimes we offered Mr Gibbons a hot tart if we thought of it. Frances was the most generous and was usually the one who offered him something first.

This good time lasted for two years and I became more and more interested in all that we were learning. Being at the top of the school we were maturing fast and Mr Stenning sometimes sent Frances and me to help in the infant class. We enjoyed this and felt very motherly and important. In secret we put our hair up and looked in the mirror to see if we resembled the new actresses we so much admired. There had been some special "film-shows" in the village that winter. Although they were silent films we fell in love with the heroines in their various plights and longed to be glamorous and rich like them. As they reclined on sofas or fled evil pursuers up

116

rugged mountain sides — still with perfectly arranged hair and in high-heeled shoes — we felt carried away into heavenly realms. Not for us the brooms and homespuns!

The trouble was that all was not well at "The Beeches". I felt increasingly disregarded. Once we had settled into the new house everything seemed to get on my nerves. My mother, although she had always encouraged me to learn, was so busy and distracted by the new farm affairs she seemed to have no time for me except to help her with the work. She overruled everything I said and if I tried to answer back she lost her temper and shouted at me. She treated me like a child yet expected me to work like an adult and she was quite impervious to my growing tender feelings. One day she summoned me for a job when I was looking at some of my new postcards (picture post-cards were all the rage among us schoolgirls). When she saw me hesitate she snatched the postcards from my hand and threw them in the fire. I was furious and stormed out of the room and we did not speak to each other for the next twenty-four hours. I did my tasks grudgingly and in rebellious silence. "I wish I didn't live here!" I sobbed in my pillow at night.

I almost began to dislike the endless round of milking cows, poultry-keeping, the muck-spreading and the carting of huge loads by the straining horses. The everlasting soughing of the wind in the beeches began to irk me. It seemed always to be raining and the mud got everywhere so that we lived in leather boots, which gave me corns on my toes, and I had to take them on and off whenever we passed through the back door. Whenever the men came in they left enormous dirty boots in the scullery with the dogs, and they shouted for help or for food and drink and everything had to be ready. Often there would be two or three men to feed as well as my father and Maurice and they took over the kitchen while I tried to creep away and do other things. Girls did not count! There would be a lot of bad language and sometimes arguments. The biggest subject of contention was money. Money was so short that if anyone had a grouse about being done down or owed money there was a mountainous tirade against offenders. Similarly, stories of a bargain at the market were discussed over and over in triumphant tones.

My mother cooked pans of bacon and eggs and potatoes on the kitchen range and served sugared cups of tea from her huge pot. My father, who had a moustache, usually tipped his tea into the saucer and drank from the saucer. There were always clothes drying, draped on the horse round the fire after mangling so that the kitchen was crowded. When the men were out working in the rain they threw sacks over their head and shoulders and turned their caps backwards and their hair and beards were always full of bits of straw which I had to sweep up in the kitchen. In the midst of all this nobody took the slightest notice of me except as an extension of my toiling mother. Any learning or imagination I showed was ignored by the men, especially Maurice who jeered at my efforts to discover the outside world through books or by discussion of anything. Consequently I kept my interests to myself and shared them only with Frances in private.

I also began to dislike my clothes. They were thick and old-fashioned and the rain and the mud meant that we could rarely wear anything pretty. My Aunt Kit, my mother's older sister, was a professional dress-maker in Southampton and whenever she visited us, which was rare, she wore beautiful clothes, silks and cashmere shawls or satin blouses trimmed with lace, and Arnold her son wore a smart sailor-suit. She wore fine-knit stockings and pointed shoes whereas we wore thick hand-knitted wool stockings. I envied her and wished she would take me to see Southampton to visit the big shops. But on her visits Aunt Kit was blessedly interested to hear me express my ideas and once we talked about fashions. She told me how people could buy ready-made cheap clothes in some shops instead of paying proper dressmakers but they secretly cut the labels off so that nobody would know that they came from the cheap shops. "But you always know," she scoffed, "because they fit so badly!"

Sometimes I escaped to the village on the pretext of an errand for the household. One day when the sun was shining I put on my new hat and was off before my mother could waylay me. I fancied myself in this hat which had been a present from an older cousin. It had a green ribbon round it and little pink flowers and Ethel James had greatly admired it. I knew my mother would disapprove but I felt it would impress some of the people in the village. When I reached the church gate I paused hoping I might meet my friend Rosa but she did not appear. The stone angels on the west tower looked fixedly above. I strolled on and watched the blacksmith placing a red-hot shoe on the hoof of a great shire-horse. I liked the smell of the smoke that rose in a cloud from the singed horn and the hiss of the iron as he plunged the hot shoe into the water tank. If the horses flinched or moved the stream of bad language from both carter and blacksmith was as fiery as the furnace and we were not supposed to loiter round the smithy. But I was drawn by a kind of fascinated horror. Of course everything we did got back to my mother, village tittle-tattle travelled fast. It was known by everyone if you had walked along Chapel Row or bought a bun at the baker's shop or peered through the door at the Queens Head. This day I felt I did not care if anyone *did* see me outside the blacksmith's shop. Let the nosey-parkers tell my mother, I didn't care!

I walked on down the street hoping people were noticing my hat and looking out for friends. I felt very superior as I ordered half a pound of Lipton's tea at the shop and saw the assistant eyeing my head. He smiled as he took my sixpence and I paraded down the street head in air towards some women who were gossiping at the corner. They stopped talking and gazed at me as I passed. Then I heard one of them say: "She bean's no che-ild no more, she be-ant, a-stucked up ther' in that fancy hat others." Indignation and satisfaction tore at my heart as I continued on my way. They were as bad as my mother the way they resented anyone looking attractive! On the other hand they did recognise that I was becoming grown up and I felt partly mollified by that.

On the way home I took off my hat and hid it under my coat. As I reached the back door of our house my mother appeared. "Wherever have you been?" she said, "you haven't fed the hens! And there's a whole pile of mending waiting to be done." . . .

CHAPTER
TWENTY-FOUR

A New Opportunity

In the autumn when we climbed as usual up the hilly lane and road from school, the hedges would be nearly blown clear of leaves. Only the silvery tangle of Traveller's Joy lay deeply along the top. Under this for a moment there would sometimes be a bustling of things unseen and all at once the air would be full of birds flying. They would scatter in a cloud, darkening the air and filling the spaces between the hedges with the pulse of beating wings and shrill crying. Then they would disappear suddenly into the hedge again in front of us and the rustling would begin all over again until the hedge ended. Then suddenly they would all fly away into a big wych-elm in the middle of the field nearby. They were autumn chaffinches, become bachelors, casting off the cares of family life and congregating in flocks to live in a commune — a kind of Jekyll and Hyde existence. For half the year the chaffinch is a minstrel and a lover and for the latter half he fraternises and forages all day long, having packed his wife off to live with other chaffinch wives over the winter. It amused me to watch them, and this autumn they were back again.

I was by now thirteen and so was Frances. I knew that when we were fourteen we would leave school like everyone else but what would we do then? Some girls went out to work as servants or dairy-maids but our parents would not have dreamt of us doing that. We would probably do what most girls like us did — help our mothers at home. Girls helped their mothers or relatives on the farms and joined in the general activities of the village, hoping that eventually a suitable boy would appear and transport them to homes of their own. Otherwise they would remain in the house and gradually take over the duties while looking after the group of ageing or sick parents and relatives who congregated in every family household. Such a stultifying existence was abhorrent to me and I was determined to seek out an alternative. How could I escape? There was only one remote possibility. It was to teach. Frances and I had quite enjoyed helping the little ones at school and this might be a way forward if it was allowed to continue. But would they take two of us as teachers at Batcombe? And if not, how did one become a teacher in another school if one did not already know the Headmaster or have links with that village? I could not imagine any of them would want us at 14 and they certainly would not pay us.

"They won't let us," Frances said. "My mother says that from now onwards the government is going to have only teachers who have been trained in college in our schools and so they will have to pay them more." This was a blow. I understood that people only went to college who were very clever and also very rich. Also they were all over eighteen. It was quite out of our reach "What shall we do?" I asked Frances.

"Let's ask Mr Stenning," she suggested.

A few weeks later, as I returned home from Upton Noble one day, I found Mr Stenning, our Headmaster, in our kitchen talking to my parents. "Norah, we want to talk to you," he said. I was surprised and somewhat embarrassed. "Mr Stenning has a suggestion about your future," said my mother, "so listen."

"We have noticed at school that you have done well in teaching the little ones, and your school-work is good," said Mr Stenning, "so I have suggested to your father and mother that you take up teaching." Me! Take up teaching! Had I heard correctly? He continued, "The government has a new plan to encourage women to be teachers. They are willing to pay the fees at certain senior girls' schools if pupils reach a sufficiently high standard, and if they do well pupils would then proceed to college where again their tuition fees would be paid." College! Impossible! What school would I go to? There was no such place in Batcombe or Evercreech.

"You have heard of Sunny Hill, the new school for girls in Bruton?" Yes! I knew of a girl in Batcombe who went there. She lived in a grand house.

"They are implementing this scheme at Sunny Hill and your parents and I have decided you should go there. They have accepted my recommendation for a place for you."

Me, at a smart girls' school! Would I know what to do? Wouldn't the work be very difficult? I felt bewildered. "How would I get to Bruton?" I asked my father, who did the driving. It was five miles away and a very hilly road.

"You would have to be a weekly boarder and come home just for weekends," my mother answered for him. "We shall have to pay the boarding fees but that is the only way we can do it."

Boarding! The word filled me with dismay! I had read Jane Eyre and Sarah Crewe and the very word filled me with alarm. I had never been away from home before and how would I survive such hardships?

"Boarding is not like it used to be," contributed Mr Stenning kindly. "Schools look after you, nowadays, and they make sure that you are well and happy. Sunny Hill is new and very modern and there are nearly eighty girls there. I hear very good reports of the school. They have excellent teachers, many of them from the university, and the girls do wonderful work. The Headmistress is Miss Radford and she has built up the school since 1900 so that now it is becoming as well-known as Kings School and Sexeys. You are fortunate to be accepted." Kings and Sexeys were the two magnificent boys schools in Bruton and I began to be half excited as well as half afraid.

"When would I have to go there?" I asked.

"In the autumn when the new school year begins. Frances is going to be a boarder at the school as well." Neither Frances nor I had heard of this plan but we did not expect to be consulted over what was considered good for us. We did as we were told by our elders and betters. But we had never encountered such a momentous decision as this!

As soon as I knew that Frances was going to Sunny Hill too some of my fears receded. We would embark on this adventure together and who knew what the future might hold? My mother and father seemed to have decided my immediate future with Mr Stenning so there was nothing more to discuss. I said, "Thank you" to Mr Stenning but remained foolishly tongue-tied while he finished his cup of tea and prepared to depart. "This will be your last term at school," he said to me finally, "and we will give you more help with your work. Then away to boarding-school!" He smiled kindly as he passed the door.

The next morning Frances and I rushed to find each other. What would it all mean? "We've got to be boarders!" I said tremulously. "My mother says that's good," Frances insisted, "because if we go to college we'll be used to living away." "But think of all the clothes we'll have to buy, they wear special uniform at Sunny Hill." "Yes, they do 'gymnastics' in special short tunics and they play hockey!" We stared at each other in dismay.

The rest of the term passed in a mixture of excited plans and of dreaded departures. Frances and I wrote extra compositions for Mr Stenning and spent extra time with the infants. At last the moment came when we all said good-bye to our friends, to Edith and to Mr Stenning. I felt quite sad as I saw their kindly faces and the rows of wooden desks in the old schoolroom for the last time. It had absorbed nine tumultuous years of my life and it was hard to imagine no longer being part of it. We promised to come back and visit them and tell them about Sunny Hill.

As we walked out through the playground in the afternoon sun on the last day the air was warm and serene. The Mendips in the distance looked blue and gentle and hardly a cloud could be seen. A song-thrush was trilling on a nearby tree in the churchyard.

"How I love this place," I thought. "Must I really leave it for an unknown future?"

CHAPTER
TWENTY-FIVE

The New School

The day came for me to begin my career at Sunny Hill. I was trembling with nerves and excitement as I put on my new green tunic, white blouse and black stockings. My fumbling fingers made a poor job of the green tie but eventually the knot was in place and I could admire my modern appearance in the mirror. My trunk was in the hall. It was full of new equipment which I knew we could not afford, for the debt from the house still hung over us, but my mother had managed somehow. Most interesting to me were the "gym-shoes". These had rubber soles and made no sound when you walked. Rubber was a new product and I had never seen it applied to shoes before. There were new dresses and petticoats for evening wear and a great many pairs of "knickers". I felt wonderfully emancipated in these and had shown them to an admiring Ethel. The knickers were dark green and had elastic above the knees while underneath we were to have separate white lining-knickers which could be more easily laundered than the serge green ones. Everything was marked with name-tapes hand printed N. K. CLACEE in black indelible ink on strips of white tape cut by me.

128

On top was my hockey stick which Maurice had seized with whoops of joy and had rushed out to find a potato to hit round the yard and had made it muddy. The furious row over that had been exacerbated by his putting on my new pork-pie hat which we were listed to wear on wet days. "You'll look like those Nightingale nurses," he jeered. "Shut up!" I had shouted and had flung the hat back in the trunk onto the Bible and pen-nibs which lay carefully packed at the top. All these were now locked inside and my straw boater hat with its green ribbon and badge was ready above it.

I could not eat much dinner. My father had gone to catch the pony ready for our journey and was missing at the table. After a while we heard him shouting for Maurice. "That dratted pony won't come, we'll have to drive him in!" he swore. But Punch, the new gelding, was too cunning. After a while they both reappeared, red and exasperated and called my mother. "You'd better see if you can catch him. He just slips by and gallops off," they complained in disgust. My mother knew their impatience. Men always rushed and shouted at horses and never allowed that they might be nervous. Time was running out and my anxiety was increasing with every delay. Supposing I was late on the first day? Seizing a handful of oats my mother hastened down to the field and quietly talked to the wild eyed animal. Soon her hand was on his neck as he lipped the proffered oats and she slipped the halter gently over his nose and ears. With relief he was led in and put between the shafts. My mother got no praise for her patience, but I was hugely relieved to see my trunk heaved on board at last.

The journey to Bruton went all too fast behind the penitent Punch and as we made our way up the narrow high street I saw other traps and gigs arriving with heads in school hatbands visible on board. I eyed them apprehensively. They all looked very confident and clever as they turned in at the school gates and swept up the drive.

Although the Kings School Bruton was a very old foundation, Sunny Hill for girls had only been open about ten years. It was a long building covered with creeper set in acres of beautiful grounds. A fine tulip tree stood on the lawn and I was pleased to see Glastonbury Tor and the Mendips even more clearly than at home. My father tied the pony to a ring in the wall and off-loaded me at the door. Then he said a brusque goodbye and was off. I tried to look confident but tears of loss and anxiety were not far away. What should I do next? At that moment Frances arrived. I recognised their pony and my relief was inexpressible. Frances was courageous and she was never at a loss for words. "Come on," she called "Let's ask someone where to go." We entered the front door together.

A pleasant member of staff greeted us and she called a tall senior girl to show us our dormitory. "Your trunks will follow soon," she promised. The girl took us upstairs to a large spacious room with rows of beds beside each of which was a "cubicle". This was a pair of curtains hanging from a hoop which was suspended from the ceiling. When drawn the curtains made a white tent inside which one dressed and washed. Each cubicle had a chest of drawers with a jug and basin on top and a pail below. "Warm water has to be fetched from the bathroom in these big china jugs," said Cicely, our guide. There was a row of flush lavatories in the bathroom, also wash basins and a bath and, best of all, there was gas lighting. The latter had not reached Batcombe and we still did everything by oil-lamps at home. "If you're quick the water comes out hot," explained Cicely, "but if you're last, it comes out cold." Our newly acquired tap water was only cold at home so I was not worried by her warning, but we laughed politely. Cicely found our beds which were in the same dormitory, fortunately.

She then showed us some of the classrooms and the sewing room. "Miss Radford says she hopes we shall soon have a proper art studio," she said. I pricked up my ears. Miss Radford was the Headmistress and she also taught art and I longed for real art lessons. "Miss Radford's going to talk to us after tea," said Cicely and she led us into the big new refectory. We were too shy to talk much but the other boarders seemed friendly and cheerful as they started excitedly into their first bread and butter and ham of the term. I noticed a table full of staff members, the central one of which I knew was Miss Radford. She had said grace before we sat down.

At the end of the meal she stood up and a hush fell over the room. She was short and stout and she peered at us through thick round glasses. After welcoming us all, including newcomers, she continued, "You girls," her voice rose, "have wonderful opportunities today such as your grandmothers would never have dreamt of." And she outlined some of the recent successes of girls at the top of the school or who had already left to take up dazzling careers. She had a kind face and a very vigorous manner. She made us feel there was an exciting world "out there" if we were prepared to work and behave ourselves. If we did not comply we might expect fearsome retributions but the emphasis was definitely on encouragement rather than punishment — a relief to me who had recently read "Nicholas Nickleby". Everyone then sang the school song "Follow the Gleam" and we were dismissed. Some girls showed us the sitting-room and we went to unpack.

* * *

We began to settle in to the new regime. We were all in awe of Miss Radford but she was fair. She was also a brilliant teacher as I soon discovered in her divinity lessons. I was put in a class with girls who had mostly been at the school some years and I was afraid of their lively talk and superior brains. To my relief I found I could keep up quite well. I was too timid to make friends at first but there was always Frances to turn to in break-time and we agreed that the work was manageable, even interesting. In her opening lesson Miss Radford told us about the new discovery in Jerusalem of a hill resembling the "Place of the Skull" by General Gordon of Khartoum. She had a relation who was a missionary in the Holy Land and he had actually seen this skull-like rock-face and the tomb in a nearby waste patch and he thought it quite possible that Jesus was taken there. I had never thought of Jerusalem as a real place on earth and I

132

was gripped by Miss Radford's realistic description of the Resurrection story.

There were other good teachers such as Miss Stoodley, my form-mistress, who taught us history and current affairs. She had curls on top of her head. At last I began to understand the relevance of the past to the present crisis in Europe involving Germany and Serbia (which I had read about in our paper at home). She told us how the Germans had always been looking for access to the sea in the south through the Balkans and this was why there was trouble. Miss Odling, who taught us science, had her hair in a bun which sometimes fell down embarrassingly when she wrote on the blackboard, but she was patient with my ignorance of chemistry and I slowly caught up. "You have to learn your notes by heart," said Pearl in the desk next to me.

Two other teachers, Miss Cox and Miss Underhill were strict and young but they were musical, and helped the violins in the school orchestra as well as teaching our classes. Miss Underhill taught gymnastics and games which I found difficult and did not know how to handle my new hockey stick. Miss Carey, who taught mathematics, had a sarcastic, quick humour which was entertaining until it turned on you. "I think Norah Clacee was born with only nine fingers," she said one day. I found it impossible to follow her maze of instructions and she was never able, with her Cambridge academic brain, to get alongside those of us who couldn't follow. She teased me and cajoled in vain and I became more and more tense as the term wore on. Ultimately she decided I was not worth her attention and I was ignored from then on. I had to get help from a mathematical girl called Evelyn, and eventually I managed quite well, but I never managed to like Miss Carey. Yet she was wonderfully good-looking and had the most vivid green eyes I had ever seen and she wore short skirts which was daring.

There were many domestic staff in the school and our meals were served in the refectory by maids in white aprons and lace caps. Most of them were local Bruton women and I noticed how kind Miss Radford was to them, especially to her own maid, Rachel (who returned the kindness by reporting all our misdeeds I discovered later). She treated them all with respect and courtesy — all except one, the matron. Our matron, Miss Thompson, was very tall and straight, a qualified nurse of distinction who guarded her patients with possessive care. There seemed to be a perpetual tension, however, between her and Miss Radford. It was a battle for authority.

One day we were assembling for prayers. The whole staff and Miss Thompson had to attend prayers together with the boarders in the dining-hall each morning before eight o'clock breakfast. Miss Radford, short and stout, swept in past Miss Thompson, tall and straight, and we had to guess whose word would be law that day, the "high" or the "broad". We repeated our prayers with Miss Radford and then came the time for notices. "Juniors who have free-time before supper," said Miss Radford "may play in the garden beyond the sewing-room unless it is raining."

"I'm sorry Miss Radford, but they can't do that," rang out Miss Thompson's voice from across the room. "That garden is right underneath the sick-room and I can't have girls who are ill disturbed by juniors playing just outside."

Miss Radford paused. Then, with great presence of mind, she resumed her authority "Juniors will play in the yard outside the art-room, in that case, which is underneath my window and if you make too much noise, which I am sure you will not, I shall open my window and tell you so. Note how well you are cared for, all you girls. You are fortunate to have a matron so particular for your well-being when you are ill." She did not look at Miss Thompson but walked straight past her and out into the hall where she collected her letters and went to her room.

It was a principle at Sunny Hill that girls should be as healthy and full of fresh air as possible. To us from cosy farm-kitchens this was a shock. Breakfast in summer was a chilling daily experience. With the French doors open to the Mendip winds, big bowls of greenish rhubarb lined the long trestle tables in the dining-room. Until you had swallowed your portion of this sour concoction you were not allowed to proceed to your bread and butter. Was it a decision of the head or the matron that we should suffer so? We never knew. But it marred the start of each day. The rest of our food, although plain, was wholesome enough. There were stews and boiled suet-puddings and rice puddings in particular, but always meals were served with home-grown vegetables or salad from the garden. Sunday lunch was considered the high-point of the week, but as

I always went home at weekends I missed that treat. I still longed for Saturday mornings when I could walk round the farm and be my old self again.

CHAPTER
TWENTY-SIX

Saffron

Country people kept well on the whole, if they had good food to eat and a warm house in winter, but medicines were popular and herbal remedies in particular. Meadowsweet was infused to cure headaches, for example, and peppermint leaves for indigestion. Every spring my brother Maurice and I had to suffer a teaspoonful of brimstone and treacle each day before breakfast for a week. It was said to clear the blood. People drank camomile tea for colds and it was comforting if you were feverish. Wild plants were all understood and prized.

One evening I met an old woman in our top field. Summer was nearly at an end and the hay had been carried in from the water-meadows and there wafted all around the fragrance of the newly-made ricks.

In the distance, wandering to and fro in my father's meadow which had been created from five acres of woodland, she seemed to be mushrooming, stooping every now and then to gather something.

I called out to her: "What are you looking for over there?"

"Crocuses," she answered. She got up from her work with a look of surprise on her face and came hobbling across to me.

"Good afternoon. 'Tes a beaudiful fine a'lternoon," said she, as if to draw my attention from the crocuses.

This was old Nancy Cox, a little wrinkled gimlet-eyed grandmother in a blue sunbonnet and holding her grey apron bunched up in one hand. I agreed with her about the weather. She nodded her head thoughtfully and with an air of satisfaction, added "Zo 'tes."

"What are those bulbs for?" I asked, taking one from her apron.

"Medicine," she replied.

"What will they cure?"

"That, now, I couldn't a-swear to. They do tell I, they do use them for the gout and for the bronchitis. But I wouldn't a-tell 'ee wrong, mind, for to lead 'ee astray."

"I suppose you will sell them to a chemist?" I asked. Nancy gave me a quick glance then looked up at the blue sky and cogitated.

"I couldn't rightly say what the man do. No! I couldn't. Maybe he do be a chemist, maybe not."

"But isn't it printed at the top of his letter?" I persisted.

"I be'ant no scholard myself, I bean't. I do carry the bulbs into town and a friend do zend 'em off fur I. He reads the letter for I when it comes. 'Tes terrible wrong to zay more 'an you do know — zo 'tes."

A few yards away a small group of full-blown blossoms peered about the short he-grass. Of a pale mauve with five petals springing from an even paler tube, the meadow-saffron is the most delicate of all autumn crocus flowers. No leaves protect it — they have gone before the flower appears. It flowers just before the autumn frosts and withers away without revealing its seeds. The ovary lies hidden under the ground at the very bottom of the tube for the duration of the winter. In spring, seed, stalks and leaves spring up together. The seeds mature and drop, the leaves wither and disappear before the lovely saffron flowers of next season pattern the meadow.

"But you have missed those," said I, pointing out an early group.

"Oh they be no good," said the old lady. "They'll write and grumble to I if I do zend many that be in full flower. Just a peep is enough, else there isn't the strength in 'em."

She now walked over to the solitary little group and forked it up, addressing the poor flowers in terms of derision:

"You be too fast by half," cried she, holding the bulbs up to strip their petals. "I suppose you fancied yerselves most terr'ble, didn't you, a-stucked up there zo wonderful and fine afore all the rest o' yer own sort? Zo now you be a-digged up, zo ye be. I didn't ought to put you in. There, 'tis but a few — they'll never hook they out! Though 'tes wrong, I do know zo 'tes." She dropped the long-suffering bulbs into her apron.

"No, no," she added "They will not have 'em in flower zo I squint and poke about to find 'em the very minute they peep above ground."

It was an open-air pursuit and gave all the pleasures of searching. Thus the gloaming came creeping on before Nancy gave up squinting and poking.

"You will send them to London?" I asked. The old soul looked crafty. Then she said:

"Now I couldn't rightly say, for I be no scholard. Good ni-eet!" She knew and I knew that this was my father's field from which she was profiting, but we both went on our way.

The meadow-crocus only grows in very sheltered places and it takes hundreds of them to create one single ounce of saffron. The unhappy fate of these lovely "naked ladies" seemed to signify the end for them, for as grass planting progressed on our farm, their delicate mauve patterning of the meadow disappeared altogether. The machines which spared the toil did not spare their natural grace.

CHAPTER
TWENTY-SEVEN

A Hard Winter

There followed one of the worst winters I could remember and we always had hard winters in the Mendips. The January skies had been leaden for days on end. On the high ridges around Priddy, with its desolate barrows, the snow had been so deep that hundreds of the sheep had died. The winding dry stone walls up there had not been sufficient to protect them, especially on the wind-swept northern slopes, and some ewes had even dropped early lambs when the blizzards struck, so they were especially vulnerable. Sheep can survive quite well in snow and the Mendip farmers knew it. They will form a phalanx, huddled together, and the snow will form a roof as if over a house. Inside this their wool and their breath keep them moist and warm, provided they don't stifle. But they cannot last long without food and the blizzards had made the tracks impassable on the higher slopes. As the shepherds struggled to find them, the sheepdogs could hear their muffled bleats but could not always reach them.

For us the snow provided a challenge and excitement. "You'll never get that old pony up your hill!" a friend called Evelyn had mocked at the school door as Maurice came to fetch me on the Friday afternoon. "Of course I will," shouted Maurice and with a touch of the whip we cantered dangerously along Bruton High Street to the alarm of the women hurrying home with laden baskets in the whirling snow. When at last we ploughed through our hilltop gateway I knew I would not see school again for some while. We had been swallowed up in a new white world.

Then the skies cleared and the frost arrived. At Batcombe the lake at Sole Bottom froze hard and some of the big Coney family from Kings Hayes had appeared with their skates. They were soon joined by others from Westcombe House and from the Manor, and we went down to watch as they hissed across the polished ice kept clear by the sweepers. The ladies wore beautiful furs and the men laughed a lot as they escorted them. Two local gallants waved their hats as they attempted to jump a row of logs and then collided with the plump nursemaid from the Rectory and fell in a heap . . . "Ho! ho! young sirs, not so fast!" she cried, as she gathered her skirts together. They picked her up and danced her round the lake and soon she was all smiles again.

One evening they danced by the light of little coloured lanterns placed round the lake while a band played Sir Roger de Coverley. A great fire was lit on the banks and a whole sheep was roasted and brightly lit stalls appeared laden with drinks and hot pies. We young ones tramped to and fro excitedly ignoring our frozen toes until the driving snow returned and sent everyone home to bed.

Because our farm was high up above the village we received the brunt of the snow and the roads were very treacherous. My father had taken the pony to Bonds, the blacksmith's in Wanstrow, to have his shoes roughed, but even with the new spikes his feet could not hold the cart and the whole lot slithered into the ditch. The cart was left there, soon to be buried in snow, while they cut the traces and led the pony home to the stable. It had cost my father sixpence to have the spikes put in (and a further threepence to have them later removed) and as a whole round of new pony shoes only cost two shillings he felt he had got the worst of the bargain, since the snow stopped all activity. The Bond brothers, William and Harry, were good-natured and could do anything.

As well as shoeing horses they were carpenters and wheelwrights, and later when the thaw came they were called in to mend bridges and fences wherever the storm had struck. They helped us mend the wheel of the cart which had twisted. "Looks like thee put the cart before the 'orse, Mr Clacee!" called Henry. "When shoes don't hold a horse, even when they're roughed, you have to do the best you can," retorted my father.

"Ah, we'll give 'un a set o' they ice-skates next time," promised Harry, and he laughed very loud and spat on the deadened grass.

Meanwhile, our animals were crowded into sheds and pens and even there icicles hung down on their whiskers. The geese, deprived of exercise, were silent, huddled together in the straw in the corner of their shed. Apart from the ganders they were kept for their eggs and not for the table and some of them were quite old — one was

143

well over twenty — and they resented being restricted by the frozen door. But they were safe. We saw the footprints all around in the snow of the hungry fox and vixen and we could not forget that in broad daylight they had carried off two of the best layers the year before, leaving just their heads behind as witness. Milk from the cows froze in the pails before it reached the dairy. The water pumps were frozen. While Father and Maurice laboured by lantern light with the milking and animal feed I fetched coal and logs for the kitchen range, wrapped in old shawls and with sodden leather boots. My mother cooked and scrubbed freezing pails and tended the poultry as best she could and none of the farm helpers could reach us.

We were not short of food but we had no bread. The baker who normally called with his cartload of white loaves (and sometimes doughnuts or a treacle tart) could not reach us, so my mother made Welsh cakes until the flour ran out. After that we lived on porridge and potatoes, to Maurice's disgust.

The thaw came at last and with it a torrent of disasters. Trees which had been split open by the frost stood like broken sentinels in the swirling flood waters. Dead sheep and cattle were washed under the river bridges and several cottages in the village which had thatched roofs had caved in under the weight of snow. An old couple who were struggling to keep out of the Workhouse had died of the cold and nobody knew it because their cottage was too remote to reach. There was so much to clear up it seemed as if troubles would last forever.

* * *

But Easter came at last, the roads cleared and everybody was relieved. It was time for me to go to school again.

We were not the only ones to have experienced trouble. When I returned to school everyone's conversation centred on the *Titanic*. There had occurred the worst maritime disaster ever known and people could hardly believe the reports that flooded the front pages of the newspapers. As the new term began Miss Radford gave us a long talk, explaining how the tragedy had occurred.

"The ship was so big it was like a magnificent floating hotel with every luxury you could ever imagine available on board," she said. "Because it was so wonderfully designed it was assumed to be unsinkable. Sailing ships might go adrift in the gales but not the *Titanic*! With its powerful engines the *Titanic* could go where it liked and negotiate anything. So with nearly three thousand wealthy passengers on board the vessel had set sail on its celebration maiden voyage to America. But then it ran into disaster near Newfoundland. The people on board were eating and drinking and dancing and enjoying themselves and they did not know that there was a huge ice-berg just ahead because it was night-time. They ran straight into it and the water poured through a hole in the bows. There was no time to warn everybody. Those that could rushed for the life-boats and the women and children were put into them. It was bitterly cold and some were only wearing evening dresses or nightdresses. The men all stayed on board,

145

together with the captain of course, because there weren't enough life-boats for everybody. And — oh dear — it is feared they all drowned."

Here Miss Radford paused, as if overcome, and we were silent, not knowing how to assimilate such a picture of horror. Then she continued "Reports say that over 1,500 people have died in this terrible event and I know that you girls will be as deeply shocked as I am to hear about it." Frances had read about it in her paper at home. "What was so dreadful was to hear the terrible screams as the ship went down, the survivors said," she reported to us in private. "But what was even more dreadful was the silence that followed. They would never, never recover from it all their lives even though some have got home by now."

"Why didn't they have more life-boats?" asked somebody. "They didn't think it could ever sink," said Frances.

Each morning in the refectory before breakfast we had prayers for those who had drowned and for the survivors and their families. Miss Radford told us that the governments were going to set up an International Ice Patrol to warn ships in future of such dangers as floating icebergs. "Alas, it will not help these victims," she said, "but it might help others who will follow." We talked of the ship's horrors for many days.

Once the term got under way there were more cheerful topics. The new science-block on the south side of the school was nearly built and would have gas-powered Bunsen-burners for our chemistry lessons. Also the school office where Miss Radford now employed a secretary, would soon be acquiring its very own telephone which would allow her to speak personally to people in Frome or even Bath, instead of the usual telegram being tapped out at the Post Office. We looked forward to seeing this wonderful invention. They said you wound a handle and "rang up" and an operator heard and put you through to the other person. I would be sure to mention it casually to Maurice when I got home!

I lived in the sophisticated world of school and the rural world of home, and although I appreciated the benefits of both it was not always easy to hold the two together.

This was exemplified one day when I arrived home from school one Friday with my suitcase of homework and in my uniform as usual. As we drew up to our farm gate I dismounted and Maurice speedily took the pony away to the stable. This was always a tense moment for me because of the geese and Maurice knew it. If they were near the gate they would fly at us, cackling wildly. If they were away down the field one might slip through quickly before they raised the alarm. The gander was with them and he was particularly fierce and only my mother could withstand him. This time they seemed to be absent so I took my chance, opened the gate and began to creep across the paddock. I was half way across when I heard the dreaded sound and the whole flock raced from behind a hen-house where they had been resting, necks extended and wings beating. Terrified I fled to the house, just in time to slam the garden gate but not before my school straw boater had slipped off my head and lay white on the grass. I daren't go back. The geese surrounded my hat and then the gander stretched out a long neck and turned it over. He obviously liked the look of the straw for in a short time he picked it up in his beak and walked off with it, followed triumphantly by the females. "My hat!" I shrieked, as my mother alarmed by the hubbub, appeared at the door. "Oh dear, it will be ruined," she cried. She managed to retrieve it a short while later, with a handful of corn while she collected the daily eggs, but the geese had done their worst with the straw, especially in the mud around their drinking trough, and my hat never looked the same again. I wondered what our matron would say to me.

Back at school on Sunday evening I told Frances about it and she laughed. She knew the ways of geese. For the time being I kept my hat at the back of the cupboard and Miss Thompson never noticed its battered appearance. Would she, who came from urban Bristol, believe it if I told her that the geese had eaten it?

While innovations multiplied at school, difficulties multiplied at home. The geese might have recovered from their restriction by the winter snow but it was months before our farms recuperated from the ensuing floods. The sinking of the *Titanic* in April added to the general distress. With the influenza and other illnesses which followed such a winter the year 1912 had a terrible start and many people died. We were glad when the summer came and we could think of happier things.

CHAPTER
TWENTY-EIGHT

An Experiment

It was not altogether satisfactory being a weekly boarder at Sunny Hill because I made close friends neither with boarders nor with day girls and could not enter fully into either life. But I eventually made a special boarding friend called Evelyn Horler, the girl who had helped me with the dreaded Geometry theorems, and she and Frances and I worked together as the time for our Junior Oxford examinations drew nearer. Once Evelyn came home with us for the weekend. She came from Bath and it was a special treat for her to spend a long weekend on the farm. She was tall and had brown curly hair, whereas I was short and my hair was blonde and straight. She had a soft skin and large brown eyes. She and Maurice quickly made friends and teased each other about the benefits of town versus country life. He said electricity was dangerous and she said cows were dirty. I found it rather disturbing that she seemed to criticise our way of life, but once back at school I managed to forget it, and Evelyn remained a friend.

Frances was by now our neighbour since a rich relation had died and had bequeathed her parents Eastcombe Farm which was adjacent to our land and this made me very happy. We could visit each other frequently by crossing a few fields. We talked behind the hay-ricks about school, the people we liked or disliked, our lessons, our food, the injustices we felt or the misdeeds of some of the girls in our form and their punishments. In spite of our grumbles we felt liberated by being among modern girls and women who were proud of their femininity rather than humiliated by it and who asserted their independence. Although keeping up with so much that was new made us tired, it extended our horizons and gave us a new self-confidence. I was by now nearly sixteen and felt at ease at school. Sometimes I secretly took apples or cakes for the boarders to eat in the old disused laundry room — a risky but popular gesture which had so far escaped Miss Thompson's sharp eye. I also discovered that some of the day girls lived quite near Batcombe and I was invited to a birthday party. My Aunt Kit had sent me some real silk stockings and I felt I looked like Zena Dare as I paraded to the house. But nearly all the girls had silk stockings and even prettier dresses than my home-made lace and taffeta and I suddenly felt shy and awkward in their sophisticated company. Why did we have so little money and have to work so hard at home?

One of these girls called Elsie Wheeler was older than the rest and was very kind and she talked to me. I developed a schoolgirl crush on her and followed her around. She also had a beautiful singing voice. This drew quite a crowd of admirers round her whenever she was persuaded to sing at a party. She was not embarrassed, as I would have been, to give a rendering of "Cherry Ripe" or "Where 'er you walk", and she sang with spirit. It was not surprising therefore that she was chosen for the part of Ko Ko when it was decided at school that the year's performance should be "The Mikado". I sometimes helped glorious Elsie by playing the piano for her in the music room as she practised "Tit Willow" and a group of us enjoyed our art class painting a pagoda with almond blossom against a sunset sky. The performance was ambitious and the people of Bruton flocked to see it as well as parents and friends. Miss Radford presided in the front row with the governors and we all felt pleased with ourselves. It was pleasant also to have a distraction from examinations in the middle of the summer term when everyone could feel relaxed and cheerful. I quickly fell in love with Sullivan's music and hummed it all day long. It reminded me of Elsie!

At weekends I was fetched in the pony and trap, now always driven by Maurice who would soon be due himself to sit for a scholarship to Sexeys, the boys' Grammar School next door to Sunny Hill. His heart was still more in farming than in books and in confidence he assured me he reckoned he had received enough education. Although he was only twelve he was quite big and manly and organised his own life.

One day as we were climbing the hill from Bruton to Batcombe he said, "I've got a surprise." Turning the pony into a side-lane where we could be unobserved he pulled out of his pocket a little packet. It was a packet of Woodbine cigarettes (price threepence) and some matches. "Like to try?" he asked. "Of course," I answered thinking how much the girls at school would admire this devilish crime. I tried to light the cigarette in the way I had seen filmstars do it in the magic-lantern shows which now regularly came to our village. One leant nonchalantly back and allowed little puffs of smoke to waft from one's lips. The match went out. I tried again but the Woodbine only smouldered. "You're puffing out, you ought to breathe in," said Maurice. A fit of coughing followed but at last the "fag" was lit. We didn't like it at all but we pretended we were vastly sophisticated and turned to drive home with great satisfaction.

Our cigarettes were still hanging from our lips as we approached the turning into the road. At that moment a figure appeared coming round the corner from the road into the lane and walking briskly in our direction. The person carried a basket and wore a brown coat that I seemed to recognise. It was Rachel, Miss Radford's maid! Whatever could she be doing in our secret lane? Horror! I snatched my cigarette from my lips, threw it onto the floor of the trap and put my foot on it and gazed rigidly at the hedge. Had she seen or hadn't she? Maurice meanwhile smoked calmly on. "Put out your fag!" I hissed frantically. He looked surprised but complied. Rachel by this time had caught up with us and when she saw me she half smiled with narrowed eyes. "Good afternoon, miss," she said politely but I saw her eyeing the inside of the trap. Had she seen the smoke by our feet? The news would go straight to Miss Radford if she had. I was dumb with fright but I managed to mutter, haughtily, "Good afternoon Rachel, nice day," and Maurice urged the pony onwards. I saw Rachel staring back at us as we clattered into the road and I felt convinced then that she had seen the cigarettes. What would Miss Radford say? Would I be punished? I shared the awful truth with Maurice — I might be expelled!

Maurice shrugged his shoulders. "What does it matter?" he said "you were out of school anyway."

"Yes, but I was still in uniform."

"Oh well, you'll see on Monday," he said, unsympathetically, "and perhaps she didn't see anyway." He did not feel any blame for my predicament. I spent a miserable weekend. I could not think of anything except that maid, and Miss Radford's authoritative face loomed up in my dreams. Even when Frances called to lend me a book I felt no better and we whispered together over the field gate. I dared not say a word to my mother and Maurice was out helping father on the farm. He would drive me back on Sunday evening. Perhaps Miss Radford would be waiting for me?

Nothing happened back at school on Sunday, and no word came on Monday. I began to feel relieved but I was careful not to pass any room where Rachel might see me. Tuesday also passed uneventfully. But on Wednesday there was a message. "Miss Radford wants to see you." So all was revealed! My heart beat fast and my breath hardly came at all as with leaden feet I climbed the stairs and knocked at Miss Radford's door.

"Come in," she called and there she was at her desk with Rachel placing a tray of tea at her fireside. I stood, trembling, my eyes on the floor.

"Ah Norah," she said briskly, "just come and sign this paper. I have to send in the names of girls who are to be pupil-teachers and I seem to have lost your form."

So Rachel had not seen! I glanced in her direction but she gave no sign of recognition. She then went silently out and shut the door.

"That's good," said Miss Radford kindly as I signed the form. "I hope you are enjoying your work? That was an excellent picture you were working on last week, I hope it turns out well." Miss Radford taught us art as well as divinity and she had been particularly helpful in showing us the rules of perspective. I had been painting a still-life group in water colours.

"Yes, thank you, Miss Radford," I murmured hoarsely and I fled from her room. I was free! I had not been seen! I could live again! I rushed to tell Frances and the other girls who had relished the details of my awful suspense. "That was a jolly narrow escape!" they all agreed sympathetically.

I remained subdued for a while and wrote extra-long essays for homework, determined to take life more decorously and seriously. Miss Stoodley had told us in one of our History periods, how Serbia and Bulgaria were now at war supported by Russia and Austria, one on each side, and how Germany was joining in too. It was disturbing to hear of this trouble in Europe. We tried to forget such worries and talk about things nearer home.

CHAPTER
TWENTY-NINE

The Sundew

One evening Evelyn and I were in the corner seat of the boarders' sitting room with some other girls, when Olive Parker, who came from Upton Noble, wailed "I can't get any money out of my money-box because my brother has got the key in his pocket and he has just gone to Canada!" Everyone laughed and someone said, "Better send him a telegram." Then Evelyn casually said, "You could send him a wireless message." "What's that?" asked Olive. Then Evelyn, delighted to have an audience, told us about a young Italian called Marconi who had come to England with a new machine which could send messages, not by wires as in our Batcombe Post Office, where they were tapped out in morse-code, but by radio "waves" in the air. "The sound waves travel everywhere and they can be picked up by his machine and you can hear someone's actual voice." It was "wireless" people said and you could send a message on it as far as a hundred miles. "Much better than a telegram," added Evelyn, knowingly. "Useful at sea," added Mildred whose father was in the Navy and had seen the *Titanic*. We were amazed. Scientific discoveries were happening so fast.

I felt divided when I heard about all these new discoveries. There was the motor-car, already quite established in the towns, and someone called Bleriot had even flown in an aeroplane and got right across the sea to France without falling down from the sky. Now there was this "wire-less" machine, which sounded wonderful and even Maurice was excited by such things. He was already saving up for one of the new "bicycles" — a machine with equal wheels and solid rubber tyres which would "go much faster than any pony," he boasted. Yet I had a feeling that I preferred the pony and what would happen to our farms and villages if everything worked by machine?

When the summer came every form in school went on an all day botany expedition with Miss Odling. But Miss Radford came too which meant we had to be on our best behaviour. However, it was a welcome break in the daily routine and our form's expedition was to be to Ashcott on the edge of Sedgemoor. We were to study the particular plants in that wetland area. The day dawned dry and sultry and the horses were already sweating by the time they reached Cole, our station. I was glad of the "mechanised" train!

It was quite a long train journey from Cole but on arrival we jumped out and walked straight across to the moors past beds of withies. We were to look for special plants and above all for the sundew. Sundews eat insects so are unusual plants. They have a scarlet rosette of leaves which are sticky and these, having trapped the insect, fold inwards and consume the soft parts of their victim. I was intrigued by these grisly details.

We found meadow-sweet and Creeping Jenny and even geranium molle but no sundew. All their leaves were shiny to hold in the moisture because in spite of the water everywhere the water is so saturated with old decayed plants that the new ones can get very little of it. "But as a result," Miss Odling said "it makes a wonderful supply of peat as we shall see." After a while, still without a single sundew, the whole party moved to a wood and we all sat down under some pine trees and started on our sandwiches. Sunny Hill was generous with its packed lunches. We were munching our ham and hard boiled eggs when a shriek went up. "Help! Ants!" Then another shriek "Ow, ow, I've got ants too! Huge ones!" "They're in my . . . !" The party rose and we hastily shook out our hats, skirts and paper bags. The ants were everywhere! "We must move," said Miss Radford, and we found a nearby oak to sit under but it wasn't as dry as the clump of pines had been. I seemed to be free of ants but worse for me was the cloud of mosquitoes. They thrive in the warm dampness and soon I was accumulating maddening itchy bumps, but I dared not make a fuss in front of Miss Radford. We were still determined to enjoy ourselves but by the time we were into our jammy doughnuts and the wasps appeared, panic set in. "Just keep quite still," said Miss Odling, but it was no good. Everyone was on the run, with cries and shrieks.

At that moment a stranger's voice was heard behind us. "What do you think you're doing here?" a large red-faced man emerged from the trees wearing a cap and carrying a gun. "Oh," said Miss Radford, anxiously eyeing the gun, "this is a school expedition and we have come to study the plants. We were particularly hoping to find a sundew." "Don't you know this is private property?" he said in a rude loud voice. "You are trespassing in this wood." He glared at us. "No," said Miss Radford "we are sorry, we did not know." "All the land this side of the railway is private. I am the keeper and it's my job to keep out people like you." He watched while we bundled our possessions and scraps together. As we retreated towards the railway he called after us, "And you won't find any sundew there either."

Miss Radford and Miss Odling were clearly alarmed but once we were safely across the line we reassembled and they recovered somewhat. "Follow the paths along the ditches" said Miss Odling "and keep looking for water plants." Sedgemoor is so wet and warm there was a profusion of duckweed and crowfoot and my favourite botanical name "stagnant Potamogeton." In winter everything is totally under water so we enjoyed exploring this exposed dry world of summer and here and there were patches of heather which added colour. Many of the ditches, or rhynes as they are called locally, were bordered by willows and there were white patches of fluffy bog-cotton around them. I collected some of the cotton as padding for Maurice's birds' eggs. Still nobody found a sundew and eventually we made our way back to a cottage by the station where we had already deposited our bags and where tea was now served. Bread and butter with strawberry jam made from wild strawberries was served us by the buxom cottage owner, Mrs Cape.

On the grass at the side of the cottage there were large squares of what looked like black mud. "Those are peat turfs," explained our hostess and her husband showed us how they cut them with a special knife. When the water level dropped, he said, they took the top layer of soil which contained a great many old matted plants and their roots, and laid the pieces to dry in the sun. He showed us the finished blocks which were light brown and dry and crumbly. "These do burn slowly and well on a fire and make a wonderful cheap fuel." "Do you ever come as far as Bruton?" asked Miss Radford. "In the winter ma'am, if my old horse is still living," he smiled ruefully at a hollow-eyed brown mare dozing over the stable door. "Then I should like a load of your peat for our school," she said promptly, and he promised to come.

As there was still time before the train was due we wandered freely around picking wild-flowers to take back to Sunny Hill and bull-rushes from the ditches. The sun came out and lit up Glastonbury Tor in the far distance with mysterious shadows. Miss Odling called out "Five minutes now before the train!" and we all made for the tiny platform. At that moment a figure appeared. It was a strange man and he carried something between cupped hands. He approached Miss Radford.

"I heard you'd been sent away from t'other side," he said, jerking his head towards the forbidden levels, "and that you'd been a-looking for a sundew. They be difficult to find now and I don't rightly know if 'ee ever got one. But I've been over there myself and I've brought 'ee a sundew for to take home." Miss Odling's

159

eyes shone and we all crowded round to admire the treasure. There was the pink floret with its roots still wet and a white flower on a long stalk sticking out at the top. There was even a tiny insect struggling in its sticky hairs. The man had couched it in some dried grass and he handed it to Miss Radford.

At that moment the train came and with hastily shouted thanks we piled inside. "We'll pretend we found the sundew ourselves," suggested someone on the way home. "No, we will not," replied Miss Odling, "but we will tell them that there are kind people on the moors as well as gamekeepers!"

CHAPTER
THIRTY

The Stone-Cracker

Silas Cuff was an old man who often awakened my pity as he hobbled along with the aid of a stick from his ivy-clad cottage to his great, oblong pile of quarry stone. A farm labourer earned about 10 shillings per week but not Silas who was looked upon as a castaway from farm labour. His face was wrinkled and creased and something like a tear hung hesitatingly in one watery eye. His trousers were strapped at the knee and his boots were tipped with iron.

Throughout the spring he could be seen daily near the finger-post at the four cross-roads on the waste-land between the road and the ditch. Here while standing up he would roll down from the pile an unbroken stone and place it conveniently between his feet. Soon, sharp and fierce, the blows began with a heavy stonehammer — its shaft being about four feet long. He would crack a big stone into pieces about the size of hen's eggs.

Of all the hard manual jobs that men worked at in those days, this must have been one of the hardest. Silas carried his lunch tied into a red cotton handkerchief. He didn't like us to stop and stare because of the propensity of the stones to jump. His finished pile of "eggs" would be about three yards long and one and a half feet in depth, piled ready for the steam-roller to come and roll these stones into a patch of road. The stone was fairly soft and creamy — as well we knew on a wet day when our boots would be splashed in sticky yellow mud. In days past the steam-roller had been the epitome of heaven to my young brother. He would suddenly disappear and after a few anxious moments I could see him ensconced high up beside the driver, pretending to be working the machinery that made the big fly-wheel turn. Then I used to run for a gateway terrified they would roll me into the ground with the flattened stones! It made the stone-cracker smile and we had become quite friendly over the years.

It was here one day in the holidays that I tried to talk to Silas as he suddenly threw down his hammer to take shelter under a holly bush nearby because of a sudden April shower. A carpet of golden celandines lay beneath our feet as we sat on a dry sandy bank, dotted here and there with clumps of primroses and violets. Sunlight lit up the distant hill as a rainbow arched the sky. I said to myself, a place so beautiful could never have been meant to be a home for such abject poverty! For a long time I had pitied that poor rheumaticky old man.

"You are out in all sorts of weather," I said by way of making a beginning. The old man chuckled.

"I can't bear to be within walls — I never could. As soon as I am up I want to be out. As soon as I'm in, I want to be a-bed. It must be terrible bad weather to pen me up."

"But don't you catch cold from getting wet?"

The chuckle grew into a laugh and then Silas began to be boastful: "I've never been bad in m' life and I'm hard upon fourscore. I've had me hardships too. We've brought up ten children — seven boys and three girls. But they all went away from here to town. They all got on wonderful well because I taught 'em to take a pride in theyselves. Although you see me on a stone-heap, I've no call to work, as they be all willing to keep me, but, as I say, as long as I can crawl, I will earn my own food. I'll not be in debt to any man, that I won't."

He got up, stepped from under the holly bush and looked around at the sky. Rain was still falling, but not so fast. So he came back and sat again and shaking his grizzled head, continued:

"Things move so quick nowadays; I'm terrible afraid the time will come when there be no more stone-crackers. Even now, some o'they stones be cracked by steam at the quarry and hauled down by a traction engine. It ought to be stopped — haul the stones down and let us crack 'em, I say. There's too much steam and hurry nowadays."

I tried to lead his mind away from this sad conclusion.

"I suppose the steam-cracker and the engine cost a good bit in labour both to make and work," I suggested. But the old man shook his head. We let the matter drop.

"I suppose if you could be twenty again, you would go to town too?" His face lit with excitement.

"Bless you, no, Missee — I love the open air too well. I like the sky over my hat. When I was young, I could plough and mow and reap and make a hedge. I could never ha' stood all day long in a workshop six days a week. You see, I took a pride in m'self and that's why I come out and crack a few stones; not to be beholden to anyone — not even my own boys. No, Miss! Give me the open air and the sun and the rain."

Towards evening, when I got back to the village, old Silas was hobbling homewards down the street and in the open door of his ivy-covered cottage stood an equally old woman expecting his approach — quite a touching picture in the fading twilight. A watchful neighbour, Mrs Susan Whitehorne was standing by her garden-gate after pickmg daffodils and I stopped to say: "I had quite a chat with that old man to-day — he's a very independent old fellow."

"Independent? Silas is very well off and brought up his sons respectable: and now they help him and nothing but right, too," she said.

"No. He told me they were willing enough — but he won't take anything off them."

Mrs Susan Whitehorne laughed. "His old woman will!" said she.

CHAPTER
THIRTY-ONE

The Dentist

In our science lessons at school we wrote notes on Darwin's "Origin of Species" which had recently revolutionised everyone's scientific thinking. I liked the arguments and Miss Odling lent me some science magazines to read at home. In spite of that encouragement, for me, the best subjects of all were English Literature and Art. By the time I was sixteen I had a good grasp of the poems of Wordsworth and Coleridge and had read the essays of Charles Lamb and Hazlitt. We even tackled modern poets like Browning and Tennyson. I had painted two watercolours which my family did me the compliment of having framed, one was a still-life of a bowl of roses, the other was of a violin on a table with china objects. I made good progress in music also, not only playing the piano at school but playing the organ in church on occasions when my teacher, Miss Davis, the village organist, was absent. I could manage the hymns and even, slowly and painfully, "Sheep may safely graze" as a voluntary. I began to feel a little superior to people in the village and adopted a "refined" accent which must have greatly irritated old friends.

One winter, about this time, an old trouble of mine reasserted itself. Toothache. I had been tormented by toothache throughout my time at school and with the Oxford exams approaching it could not have been more unwelcome. When we were little we never visited a dentist. We used to laugh at the gargoyle on Wells Cathedral of a poor man with toothache. But in our teens our own troubles began and we paid our first visits, at great expense, to one of the few dental "specialists" in Frome. My mother, who had lived in up-to-date Cheltenham for a time, insisted on a "qualified" man rather than a local "quack", so she now wrote for an appointment for me.

Until Queen Victoria's reign people in England had been unaware of the need to keep teeth clean and mended. Their teeth were left to become coated and rotten and caused continual pain. There were old folk-lore remedies for toothache like "earth worms boiled in wine" or "a frog tied round the neck" but the only other solution at that time was to take the tooth out. This was a last resort, the agony of having a tooth pulled out by a clumsy fist, without anaesthetics, being even worse than toothache! I had read in the same school history book that Queen Elizabeth I suffered agonies of toothache and it was hard for her to make national decisions while in such pain. One day her pain became unbearable but the torture of an extraction daunted her even more, whereupon the Bishop of London came to her rescue. That brave man had one of his own good teeth pulled out without flinching while she watched. The Queen then submitted her own tooth and was cured! She lived a long life but was virtually toothless by middle age and so had difficulty, it seems, in making her speeches to a turbulent Parliament.

I was thankful to live in "modern" times but I still dreaded the forthcoming dentist's visit. Instead of chipping at decayed teeth by a chisel, in 1897 when I was born, dentists had invented the "drill". This was worked by a foot pedal so that both his hands were free to grind off the decay and it saved the tooth, but it was still an ordeal.

My grandfather had told me that in his day you either suffered toothache or had it pulled out in the market-place by a blacksmith or chemist for sixpence. I had seen fearful pictures like this in a book by Hogarth at school. Consequently many people had ugly gaps in their mouths and this was why in old photographs people never smiled. Women's fans were popular at parties and balls often to hide an ugly mouth when you had pretty eyes. I had read all this with shocked interest and determined I would do better.

Because dentists were hard to reach, girls at Sunny Hill frequently had weeks of toothache and the general attitude seemed to be that one should grin and bear it. What made it worse was that we were so cold in winter. To be cold and in pain, sometimes from a monthly stomach ache as well as toothache, was a miserable state and I now experienced it. Our dormitories were not heated at all so that we sometimes had to break the ice on our waterjugs in order to wash. Many of us developed painful chilblains on our hands and feet and it was particularly hard for people who played the piano. At home if it was bitterly cold we went to bed with a hot brick wrapped in flannel and kept our vests on but no such comfort was possible at school. When we were little we had carried hot potatoes to school in our pockets to keep our hands warm and then ate them on arrival. But gloves were forbidden indoors at Sunny Hill. I longed for weekends on these cheerless winter days and hugged the tepid radiator in the classroom.

One day, we were on the games field trying to keep warm playing hockey. The game was still new to me as we had not played it in the village school. We had learnt dancing and I loved dancing and knew a great many of the folk dances by heart and I could play some of them on the piano. I also knew how to waltz and dance an eightsome reel. But when it came to team games I was a failure. Hockey was my anathema. I ran up and down the field beside large cheerful girls but I could never stop the ball hitting my shins in spite of wearing pads. Moreover being left-handed I was often put to play left wing — but with a right-handed stick in my right hand! I never managed to hit the ball to the right and one day Miss Underhill in exasperation, changed me over and I was put into goal. This was even worse. The huge goal pads came up to my neck since I was very short and the gloves were huge and fell off every time I slapped my shoulders to keep warm. That day I had particularly bad toothache and I shivered from head to foot on the frosty field. Suddenly the opposing side was upon me. In self-defence I kicked out wildly and felt an impact on my left foot. I had saved the goal! "Well done Norah," called Miss Underhill. Clasping my gloves I gazed wretchedly round. There they were coming at me again! This time I swiped with my stick and, wonder of wonders, the ball fled to the far end of the pitch! "Well done again," called Miss Underhill. I was hugely relieved. I went back to hugging my painful face. "I'd like you to play in the house-match on Monday," said Miss Underhill when the game was over. "You know their usual goal-keeper is ill." Me! Play in a hockey-match! The idea was preposterous. "Yes," she said "You did well today." Horror filled my soul and I began to invent a thousand excuses. I knew I would miss the ball and probably get hit as well and feel ashamed. Yet there was a keen player called Betty who envied me my good luck. I was filled with dismay but there was no escape.

Fortunately it was Friday and at four o'clock Maurice was there with the trap and I had rarely been more thankful to see him. "There's a letter for you at home," he said. "Who from?" I asked surprised. "From the dentist. He wants to see you on Monday." "But that's my hockey-match day!" I exclaimed. "You'll have to miss it," he said and flicked his whip at the pony.

I could hardly believe my luck! When Monday came instead of returning to school I made my way almost gladly to Frome. The dentist's waiting-room for private patients had several comfortable armchairs and, best of all, a pile of magazines and newspapers for patients to read including *Punch*. I loved the picture of laughing Mr Punch on the cover and I relished the cynical cartoons inside and we never saw *Punch* at home. As I reached for the latest copy my eye fell on the *Times* newspaper which was also on the pile. The headlines read:

169

"Austrians attack Serbia, supported by German Emperor." I wished that somebody would sort out the trouble in the Balkans but I knew that the Treaty of London, drawn up by Sir Edward Grey, had been torn up. What was going to happen now? I turned back to *Punch*, and waited to be called to the operating room.

Soon I was in the leather chair being prepared for my "crown". It was a front tooth and drilling it away was excruciating but the dentist was a friendly man, if eccentric. He kept me enthralled with grisly stories. In the old days, the dentist told me, people tried all kinds of ways to fill a gap in the jaw. They wired in dogs' teeth or even human teeth "taken from corpses, especially after battles like Waterloo," he exclaimed. "But the wire caused trouble and the teeth rotted so they tried carved ivory teeth set into gold plate." This was better but extremely expensive, so some Germans invented porcelain-china teeth, set into metal bridges and this worked quite well — except for eating. There had been embarrassing incidents at public occasions when guests of honour had been offered sticky pies! Usually they took their teeth out for meals or ate in their bedrooms beforehand. Alongside this lurid information he set my new crown over the carefully preserved stump with special refined cement. The crown was made of the new American "vulcanite" and looked so natural I found myself transformed in the mirror.

I was particularly glad about this because in our village they had started a new fashion for "dances". These were the Saturday evening events to which all the family could go and I had been attending some mixed classes in ballroom dancing in the holidays. I had begun to take an interest in some of the new bright young men who appeared there, and I wanted to look nice when the dances began. No fans for me! I sailed home with a sigh of relief and satisfaction, beside my father in the dog-cart.

When I arrived at school the next day the hockey-match was over. Betty had excelled herself in goal and our team had won. Nobody asked why I had been absent.

CHAPTER
THIRTY-TWO

The End of an Era

In the summer of 1914, when I was seventeen, rumour reached us that England was on the verge of war. Crown Prince Ferdinand of Austria and his wife had been assassinated on a visit to Sarajevo, and this was just the excuse the Germans needed to attack their old enemies, as they rallied to Austria's support. When the Belgians, who had remained neutral, were brutally attacked by them, Great Britain and France rose to their defence and on July 28th war was declared against Germany. It came as a great shock. I felt bewildered when my father came home with the news. Small knots of worried people gathered in the village to discuss the newspaper headlines. Our army would soon sort things out, people said, but it was a very serious blow for our country just emerging peacefully into the 20th Century. "It's only twelve years since they got back from the Boer War", lamented poor old Mrs Dyer.

Soon public posters were pinned up. Young men were invited to volunteer for the troops and many patriotic youths in Somerset, fired with enthusiasm, went immediately. Our anger against the Germans found an outlet in their instant heroism and towns like Frome

172

hastily commandeered halls to serve as Conscription Centres. The whole nation began to be in a state of turmoil.

When I went back to school in September there was an air of intense patriotic fervour. Some girls, whose fathers were professional soldiers, had already proudly waved them off to France. The Union Jack was flying from our flag-pole. Miss Radford gave us a serious talk about behaviour in war-time: "sober and helpful," she said. At every formal occasion we sang "God Save the King", standing very upright and solemn. Miss Radford made us learn by heart Kipling's "Recessional", written for Queen Victoria's Diamond Jubilee, and we frequently sang that too, with trembling voices:

> "God of our fathers, known of old,
> Lord of our far-flung battle-line,
> Beneath whose awe-ful Hand we hold
> Dominion over palm and pine —
> Lord God of Hosts, be with us yet,
> Lest we forget — lest we forget!"

On Prize Day, which always fell in October, it was decided that there would not be an entertainment by girls for the guests, as a sobering reminder of the war, but there would be an exhibition of work. I was glad about the exhibition as some of my drawings were included, but during the year before some of the girls who had been to a stirring lecture on the Suffragettes had performed a very clever Suffragette scene and we had hoped for some similar drama on Speech Day. Instead, the highlight of the afternoon was a Map of the War which we seniors, who did art, had prepared for the guests. It included all in the combat — Germany, Russia, Austria, Serbia, Bulgaria, Albania, Greece, Romania, Italy, Hungary, Turkey, Portugal, Japan, Belgium, France and Great Britain — but not America.

Throughout the autumn term we were encouraged to work very hard "as a tribute to our brave men who had gone to fight for our country," said Miss Radford. Lord Kitchener had appealed to the nation for volunteers and over a million of our young men had responded. Who could fail to win a war with such a gallant leader and so many fine British soldiers? Frances and I worked extra hard because we knew that our final examinations loomed the following July. From time to time we, and others, like Eveylyn, who were pupil-teachers, went out to the local infant schools and helped with the teaching and that made us feel very mature and motherly. Then we returned to school and were glad to be pupils again and to talk late in the senior dormitory about our experiences.

Miss Radford was as energetic as ever, teaching girls, interviewing parents and staff, planning new buildings for the school which, owing to her inspiration, was growing rapidly. The war was holding up new buildings while increasing the intake of new pupils — many whose families were broken up by the war situation. We were less afraid of her now that we were older and she treated us more as friends than as pupils. One day in spring she sent for Frances and me. "It is time for you to choose which College you would like to attend for teacher-training," she said. "As long as you pass your examinations you can now proceed to college and you are free to make your own choice." I had not realised this as I had imagined every teacher in our area automatically went to Fishponds College in Bristol. I felt quite excited. I had always longed to explore other new places and to escape from some of the restrictive confines of home and of Somerset village life, but how did one find out these things? Mr Stenning, my old headmaster, whom I went to consult when I next went home, had ideas. "It would be best to go to a college with a church foundation" he said. "Why don't you apply for Bishop Otter College in Chichester, which is a fine church training-college in Sussex." I had never heard of it but Miss Radford readily agreed and my application was sent off, with Mr Stenning and Mr Morant, our new Batcombe rector, given as referees.

Before long a letter came back with a provisional acceptance and my thoughts began to direct themselves towards Sussex. Surely Kipling had lived in Sussex? "You'll be nearer the war-front," said Maurice one evening enviously, "you might even hear the guns if the wind is right." "The war will probably be over by that time," said my father who was growing extra oats for the war-effort and already feeling tired.

The spring of 1915 was late, following a terrible winter. Rumours were rife. The war was not going well and there were appeals for yet more men to join up. Christmas had been bitterly cold and we heard that in France at the front there had been a gigantic thunderstorm on Christmas Eve which flooded the trenches. It then froze hard in the following weeks. Men were dying from pneumonia as well as from wounds and transport with horses was impossible in snow and ice. At sea a number of our supply ships had been sunk, and their crews drowned, by German "submarines". These wretched craft travelled underwater and were invisible until it was too late to escape their attacks and ships were being increasingly lost round our shores.

Meanwhile at home, once spring burst, the Somerset countryside was more beautiful than I had ever seen it. At school the trees blossomed and the hills were blue. It was hard to imagine a more peaceful scene and harder still to imagine the mud and horror our troops were said to be undergoing. As the warm May weather settled and the bees began murmuring in the wisteria, we were allowed to sit and study in the garden. We basked in the glory of being seniors and being scholars with important examinations. We liked the awe with which the smallest juniors regarded us. The staff had become our friends rather than our mentors and even Miss Carey, in her new plain-cut coat and skirt, was amicable. There was a new feeling in the air that women were important and that for a woman to be looking for a job was patriotic and no longer demeaning. Some women were going away from home as nurses and even as Munitions workers and we felt glad to be joining in the national effort.

Life was so busy that I had increasingly to spend weekends at school and found it surprisingly enjoyable and stimulating. But it had one unfortunate result. Sometimes when I went home I felt a kind of revulsion. Although I loved the countryside, farm life seemed

176

increasingly crude and harsh in a way I had become more conscious of. My father still ran a slaughter business and I hated it. One spring we had reared a pretty little Jersey calf whose mother was ill so we had to bottle feed him. His name was Goldie. Goldie became a pet and as a baby calf would follow us around and nuzzle us with his pink nose while his eyes seemed to smile up at us. On a summer afternoon I returned home and Goldie was dead. The butcher had skinned him and was cutting him in pieces and Maurice was helping him. I was disgusted. I was used to the hens having their necks wrung behind the hen-house but I could never get used to the butchery that farming involved. I vowed that day to escape as soon as I could.

Other things irked me also, like quarrels between my father and some of his relations who called, usually involving Maurice as well. I wished they would live in peace and stop shouting at each other. Why didn't my mother intervene or send those cousins away? But she only told me fiercely not to interfere and defended my father. A grim unyielding mood then pervaded the house and I withdrew in an angry sulk to my bedroom. The war news was worsening and that was making everyone more tense and irritable. I felt oppressed and longed to get away all the more from the confines of home.

One afternoon I walked down to the village to see what was happening there. The war seemed to make surprisingly little impact on the village in 1915 and it looked very peaceful in the sunshine. Edward Fulford stood silently by the weaver's house as I passed. He, poor fellow, gave me a reluctant nod. Our policeman had

177

gone to join the Army and there were posters in the Post Office saying "Our country needs you." The regular territorials had gone but our most serious local effort seemed to be in producing more food to send to the front. Also horses had to be supplied as well as men. There were strange stories from other villages. At Buckland Dinham, where my mother's family came from, there was a big house called Orchard Leigh. One of the ladies of the house had kept two pet dachshunds and these had now mysteriously disappeared. The feelings of the nation against anythin' "German" were so bitter that the slightest suggestion of German links in your life meant you were "tainted". A man in Frome, whose name was Bultmann had been "interred" in a special prison camp, suspected of German leanings although his family had lived in England for generations and he was as patriotic as any of us. Some families went to the lengths of changing their name if they felt they might be suspect. "If my country needs me," I said to myself, "I shall surely help by being a teacher. I shall teach the children about the dreadful way the Germans have treated the Belgians and I shall teach them to stand up straight when we sing the National Anthem." For a while I forgot the tensions at home and I joined a group at the Post Office. The young woman in front of me was posting bars of Fry's chocolate to her husband at the front. The postman having joined the army, his wife was serving everybody.

"Won't it melt?" she asked.

"It don't matter," said the woman "T'will give 'un strength for to kill more o' they German brutes. 'Ee do love 'is bit o' chocolate."

I lingered in the Post Office, pretending to have trouble with my purse. The fact was there was a young man in the village whom I had met at one of our increasingly popular village socials and had admired from afar. Once he had looked in my direction and I had been suddenly heart-smitten by his handsome smile. I used to watch for him when I was home at weekends and hoped he might talk to me. He sometimes came to the Post Office as I knew. But he had gone. His mother later told me he had joined the Territorials and gone with them to France. I imagined how handsome he would look in his uniform and secretly hoped I would see him when he came on leave. I thought about him all the way home as I climbed up our hill.

Back at school Frances and I went into our senior Oxford examination in July, with high hopes and fears. We all felt we were pioneers in education and would show our troubled nation the true value of women's minds! We left Sunny Hill in an aura of praise and honour. Miss Radford wished us all well and hoped we would uphold the honour of the school. She bid us go out and serve our country with all our might and always to remember our Christian principles.

CHAPTER
THIRTY-THREE

Troubles Old and New

It was a strange feeling not to be a schoolgirl any more. I had often longed for the moment but now that it had happened I felt at a loss. On my last drive home from Bruton in the pony and trap, with my trunk tied behind, I thought of our first days at Sunny Hill and how nervous we had been at leaving home.

Frances and I had arranged to have two extra week's teaching-practice at our old school in Batcombe and Mr Stenning gave us a warm welcome. It was interesting to see how much the school had changed under the new trained teachers. For example there was more activity but it was a creative activity. The infants were encouraged to talk more to their teacher which helped their speech, and the juniors sometimes worked in pairs. There was less learning by "rote" and more allowance for the children's own ideas in subjects like composition and drawing. They all used pencils and paper instead of the infant slates of our day. Then, if you dropped a slate-pencil it broke and you were punished and made to write with the fragments, but now these children had their own lead pencils sharpened by the teacher in a little machine. Frances and I, eager to display our Sunny Hill superiority, went from desk to desk, correcting spelling or figures, and sometimes we were brought to the front by the teacher to explain a point or to read a passage to the whole class. It made me feel exceedingly mature to be called "Miss Clacee" by the awed lips of the new infants. We enjoyed our two weeks and I began to look forward with anticipation to our forthcoming training. When I had seen the eager faces of the children I had suddenly felt "I can do this. I can make learning clear and enjoyable too." Mr Stenning encouraged us with a smile and we left with many fond farewells and promises to write letters from college.

Frances and I agreed to prepare for college and shop together in Frome. We had also arranged to meet some friends from school who, like us, were eighteen and had recently left and wanted to enjoy themselves. In spite of the war, and many of our young men going off to the front, most of life went on as usual in the country areas. We found it exciting to meet soldiers and even naval officers on The Parade in the town and there were some special concerts in aid of the war hospitals which we looked forward to. Then the blow fell. "Her teeth," said the dentist to my mother, on one of our joint visits to Frome, "are in such a bad state they are becoming dangerous. They are causing her general ill-health and it could become much worse." I had been feeling rather tired and unwell in the final term at Sunny Hill, especially as my teeth ached dreadfully. "I feel that if she is going to be a teacher," he continued, "she should have all her teeth extracted, to be on the safe side. It is hard work being a teacher and she needs all the energy she can muster." Have all my teeth out? Never! I was aghast! I would look like the witch of Wookey! I started to panic.

The dentist patiently explained that a Doctor Hunter had recently confounded the famous American dentists by proving to them that the crowns they had so triumphantly promoted were in fact "traps of deadly infection". Some of Dr Hunter's London patients who had suffered long illnesses undiagnosed, got rapidly better when their teeth were removed. He had discovered a direct connection between gum health and bodily health through the shared bloodstream. "Tooth decay can lead to illness and even death," Dr Hunter wrote in a London magazine. I was alarmed. The crown I had welcomed so gladly had indeed developed an abscess beneath and there was other trouble too. Would I really have to go through all that horror? "You won't feel a thing," said the dentist encouragingly "now that we have the new gas. And you will soon get used to dentures and they will give you peace of mind." I did not tell him that I had seen my great-aunt's dentures and the trouble they gave her. They were built on fixed side-springs, which held the top plate in place by acting like the lid of a Jack-in-the-Box. All one had to do was to hold the mouth firmly shut and there was no embarrassing slipping out which had bothered people in the past. "It's all right as long as the springs work properly," confided my aunt, as she tried to bend hers straight, "but it's dreadful if they stick!" I would not need "springs" the dentist told me reassuringly because the new plates fitted so perfectly closely they needed no support at all. I was greatly relieved. It was true the new dentures looked very natural. I certainly did not want to die of ill-health from bad teeth, so I decided reluctantly, I had no option but to have the operation. I knew that quite a lot of young people were having complete sets of dentures fitted and it was all the fashion so I would not be alone. We fixed the fateful day.

The dentist came to our house and the deed was done on our kitchen table. It seemed a fearful undertaking and I had some miserable weeks to follow, but in the end I liked the look of myself in the mirror. My smile was as good as a filmstar and it began to feel worth the temporary torture of a sore mouth. I was liberated from pain and shame! I was now glad I had "false" teeth. Ethel at Batcombe Lodge was the first to see my new appearance and she was quite envious. She had endured a great deal of trouble herself and knew no solution. There was no possibility of Ethel being in search of modern dentures and she always suffered in silence. It had been a huge extra expense for our struggling household. For me it meant release from years of distress and I could now look ahead with confidence to my career.

* * *

Lists began to arrive from Bishop Otter College. There were clothes to be bought and books to be read. We were to wear white blouses, dark skirts and the striped College tie. For gymnastics there were short dark tunics. Then there were boater hats "to be worn on all occasions outside the college grounds," said the information sheet.

The college authorities were keen that we should have plenty of exercise so that there was a Cycle Club, a Tennis Club and a Hockey Club which anyone could join. There was also pleasant walking available in the Sussex countryside and I made up my mind to explore such famous places as Bognor and Arundel. It was very exciting! I read that they had also recently built a new library with electric lighting and it housed good newspapers and periodicals as well as hundreds of books.

While I was dreaming of college and going through the last painful stages of dental transformation, work on the farm was at its peak. Haymaking followed by harvest meant that Maurice and my father never came in before dark on fine days and with only one old man left to help, my mother had to work in the fields as well. She knew how to drive the horse or stook the corn and she could fork the stooks up onto the rick like any man, but she got tired. Milking had to be kept up twice a day, as well as field-work, and my father had just built up a new beef herd. Two years previously there had been a fearful outbreak of foot and mouth disease, so that all our cattle had had to be slaughtered and burned, and every drop of milk destroyed. The government had paid only minimal compensation. The smell of the mountain of dreadful burning carcasses had dominated our lives and even now the memory haunted me. Everyone watched their new cattle anxiously and I knew my father dreaded a return of the disease. He was already in serious debt. I felt sorry for my parents' perpetual struggle and began to regard them in a new light now that I was leaving home. I determined to help as much as possible when my mouth recovered.

Meanwhile, as I was prevented from public activities, I did jobs around the house and read as much as possible. New books had to be brought for me from Frome. I read with interest John Galsworthy's new satire "The Man of Property", with its selfish, brutal Soames Forsyte and his grasping ways. I also managed to enjoy some "Ouida" yellow-backs which had been banned at school as "immoral" but seemed pleasantly romantic to me.

It was fortunate that the summer evenings were light because there was so much work to do on the farm that we were busy all day. I would slip away with my books after tea to the sitting-room which was supposed to be kept tidy and neat for visitors. The piano was in there and my mother's beautiful Copenhagen china tureen of which she was proud. She was knowledgeable about good craftsmanship and she had collected together a number of objects and figurines which were valuable, including some Lalique bowls, and she had a Royal Grafton tea-service, kept in a glass-fronted cupboard. I suddenly began to appreciate these now that I was sitting so close to them.

As I studied I would wait for the evening primroses outside the window to unfurl their yellow petals. This beautiful event happened every evening at exactly eight o'clock (because evening-primroses are pollinated by moths) and throughout August they never failed to perform. It was the signal for me to stop reading because the oil-lamps were lit at sunset and that meant moving

185

into the kitchen where there was always noise and bustle when the men came back.

One evening my father came in with angry looks and raised voice. "Two fellows from the War Ministry came," he said, "and they want all our big trees! They are going to come next week and start cutting them!" He threw out his hands in despair. "What do they want them for?" cried my mother.

"For the trenches. They said they must have all the wood they can get to make props and we have all got to supply them with trees. They will cut them up and ship them to France."

"Haven't they got trees in France?" asked my mother, distressed. "Yes, but not enough. They say we have got to help with the war and give everything we can."

"Are they going to pay us for them?" asked mother. "Not a penny," said he bitterly. "They say there will be some compensation after the war."

"We've got to win the war first," said my mother grimly, "it's taking much longer than they said at first."

"It's terrible," said father "and that's not all. They said they wanted our horses as well. They have taken all the riding and carriage horses around here, now they want the farm horses too!" I intervened at that point. "They can't want our pony, surely!" I cried.

"I said we needed the pony for transport, and that if they took the cart-horses how could I plough and reap all the extra corn and hay they want at the front?" Father threw up his hands. "They have agreed to leave them for the moment. They've taken all Mrs Ernst's horses down at Batcombe, and all the hunt horses have gone." I was dismayed. I loved seeing the horses go by, round the lanes and by-ways on our hills, and it was obvious we should never see them again. It made it worse to imagine the kind of life they would be enduring in France and the cruel sufferings of war. "I'm glad about the horses," said my mother, "but we'll have to let the trees go. We've got to win the war and do everything we can."

The next week the tree-fellers arrived and with saws and axes they cut down the whole row of beeches and the oaks as well, and their horses and our horses strained and pulled to move the great bulk to the road. Although they were seventeen hands high and fit, it took six heavy horses to move the waggons up the track and the scarred trunks went on their way. I felt that part of ourselves went with them. The beautiful beeches would simply be made into gun carriages and ammunition boxes and the oaks into pitprops, and seeing the empty patch of sky left behind them I was filled with a deep protesting anguish. What a hateful thing this war had become and how wasteful! We must stop its cruel progress! Why should so many ordinary people suffer as well as soldiers?

On the way back to the house I met Maurice with an axe in his hand. He was fourteen by now and quite tall and handsome. He had been allowed to leave school to help his father. "I wish I could go to the war," he said, looking longingly after the waggons. A sudden cold fear gripped my heart. "You are too young," I admonished him, "and anyway they need people to work on the land."

"I hope it lasts until I'm old enough," he said, ignoring my caution. "I shall go then."

187

CHAPTER
THIRTY-FOUR

College

I lay in bed listening to the owls hooting, out in our woods. There were several pairs of tawny owls up there and they lived on the voles and fledgelings that abounded in the thickets. I loved to see them swooping silently across the valley in the early morning mist, but at night their eerie calls sent shivers down my spine. I pulled the blankets over my ears. I could not sleep. It was the last night before I left for college and I was full of excitement. I recalled all the events of the day before. My mother had arranged a farewell picnic. The harvest being done we had walked up through the stubble fields to a sunny dell of grass and trees and there we lay, basking, Mother, Maurice, Ethel and Charlie who had come across from Batcombe Lodge, a couple of neighbours, Mr Stenning's daughter Dorothy, and myself, and Ruffie our dog. We ate our sandwiches and laughed together and everyone had been especially kind to me. Now the hooting owls, as I lay awake, became a comforting reminder that whatever happened in the future the woods would still be there.

At last the day dawned for my departure. As it was such a long journey it had been decided I should stay overnight at Southampton with my Aunt Kit, Mother's dressmaking sister. I felt quite tearful as I said goodbye to Mother and Father, to my surprise. Maurice and I soon set out, with my luggage in the trap, for the train. I was privately very nervous when the moment came to depart but Maurice deposited me cheerfully into my carriage and the train set off. Soon the excitement of the Dorset and Hampshire countryside in view occupied my mind and also the antics of my fellow-passengers in the carriage, several of whom were heavy smokers, and clouded the air.

After about two hours we drew in at Southampton and we all disembarked. I felt overwhelmed. I had never seen a big port before. My aunt was there to meet me. "How smart you look!" she exclaimed, admiring my new dark skirt and boater with its college band and boosting my student pride encouragingly. After taking me home for some tea she took me down to the harbour. It was a magnificent sight but very busy with soldiers, horses and baggage everywhere. To my astonishment there were two gigantic ships in port. I had never seen real ships before, only paddle-steamers at Weston-super-Mare. "They are troop-ships," explained my aunt, "going to France." I did not realise how close we would be to the war when I got to Chichester. "They bring back a lot of the wounded soldiers to Chichester hospital," Aunt Kit told me that evening. She had made me a pretty white blouse edged with lace as a parting present. She was a widow and all alone since Arnold her son, who used to wear sailor-suits and play the violin, had gone to work for Southampton Council. "You will see the South Downs on your journey tomorrow," she promised.

I reached Chichester far too early. In my anxiety to catch the right train I was there by two o'clock. "Oi' 'opes yer enjoys yerself!" said the cab-driver, in unfamiliar Sussex accents, as he deposited me at the College and drove his horse away. I gazed at the fine edifice before me. It was covered in red creeper and there were rows of delicately latticed windows between stone porticoes. The walls were golden and mellow. In the distance I could see a great cedar on spacious lawns, and a little turret crowned what looked like a chapel. So this was Bishop Otter!

Climbing the steps in the great porch I rang the bell. The door was opened by a pleasant looking elderly woman in a long white apron, presumably a housekeeper. "You are a little early," she said kindly, "but let me show you your dormitory and then you might like a cup of tea and you can look around the college for yourself." My dormitory was on the top floor and it was called Randall, "After one of the benefactors," she explained. All the beds were empty and I seemed to be the only one in the college. "The others will be here soon," she said encouragingly, and she hurried downstairs, leaving me to unpack my portmanteau alone.

After a while I wandered around feeling rather foolish. I was too shy to search out the library or the new science laboratory but I gazed down at the beautiful garden and was given my cup of tea in a wonderful large sitting room with a high carved mantelpiece over the fireplace. I began mentally to write a letter home. Presently there were voices and then a student entered the room. She said "Hullo. Are you Norah Clacee? I'm Edith McManus and I am your 'sponsor'. I have to take you round and show you everything. Let's go up to your dormitory." She had a smiling rubicund face and short wavy brown hair and together we made our way to the dormitory. Soon I met two of my new room-mates; Betty Watson and Doris Atterton. They were to become my greatest friends but for now we merely nodded and smiled. Meanwhile dozens of cheerful students began to arrive and all was bustle and noise. Even the new students were chattering by the time we gathered in the refectory for supper and I joined Betty and Doris at table.

There were a hundred students altogether, fifty in each year. "Our Principal, Prebendary Hammonds," said Edith, "has been here eighteen years and he was responsible for most of the fine new buildings". He had receding silvery hair and a moustache and wore a clergyman's white collar. He made us a speech of welcome and assured us that he was there to help us at all times and seemed very kind. His wife, as we discovered, was often about in the college helping, and his son once appeared, looking very fine in his Army uniform as he set off for France. But best of all was his daughter. Miss Hammonds had been a student at Oxford where she read English. Now she was back to share her wide knowledge with us, together with her father who would teach us divinity.

There were other resident staff who taught their special subjects such as science, geography, arts and crafts, educational theory and physical training. We met

191

them all one by one and more who came into the college daily from homes in Chichester. "They all want you to write essays at the same time," Edith told me, ruefully.

I began to make friends, especially with my dormitory companions, Doris and Betty. Doris was very short and petite, even shorter than I was, which made me feel pleasantly superior. She was going to teach infants, and she was very shy, with blue eyes and spikey yellow hair. She was not academic but when it came to doing handwork her skill was remarkable, and she would say "I might be able to help you get it right, shall I try?" whenever I muddled my stitching, and in no time everything was put right. Betty Watson, on the other hand, was very tall and angular and clever. Her long dark hair was plaited and curled round into "ear-phones" each side of her head. Her father was Headmaster of Washington School near Steyning and she hoped to be his assistant one day. She had an air of assurance, but she was also very kind and generous. Once on a walk on the Downs I tore my cardigan badly on a thorn bush and she insisted on giving me one of her own. "Keep it," she said "I have another one and I don't need two."

After a few days in college we settled down and work began. I found with relief I could follow the lectures quite well. Miss Hammonds soon involved us in Shakespeare's great tragedies and Milton's Paradise Lost, Byron's, Keats's and Shelley's poetry following next. In particular I enjoyed modern literature, such as Thomas Hardy because he was a West Country writer, but there were other modern writers to study as well, such as H G Wells. I was stirred by H G Wells and his reflections on the failures and injustices of society, as in "Tono-Bungay" and "Kipps", with its class struggles. I felt I too wanted to go out and transform some of the absurdities of English tradition after reading about them, like the treatment of factory workers before the arrival of the new trades-unions to voice their discontent.

I was inspired also by Prebendary Hammonds's insights into theology. He not only talked about the Bible but about everyday Christian life. We heard from him one day about a popular new theory, "that God Himself suffers", and discussed whether God is remote and high-above or deeply involved in our lives. It was particularly relevant because of the sufferings of war being reported daily in the papers in ever increasing volume. Can God be a loving God? We were beginning to wonder what was going wrong in the fields of France. Does God suffer with mankind and if so does it include the hated Germans as well as ourselves?

We were permitted to go into town at weekends provided we wore our hats to show we were Bishop Otter students. I enjoyed the fine old streets in Chichester and also the sophisticated shops, although I had not got the money to spend that some of the other students had. We visited the Cathedral which, although less fine than ours at Wells, contained beautiful sculptures.

There were also colourful posters in the streets inviting women to join the war-effort and work in the Munitions factories. "On Her Their Lives Depend", said one with a picture of a young woman donning factory overalls with soldiers manning machine-guns in the distance. "Enrol at once!" said another. "My brother enrolled in the first week," said Betty "when Lord Kitchener first appealed for volunteers. Now he is an officer and he's out in France in the trenches." She looked proudly in the direction of the sea. "They say there are 5,000 miles of trenches and when he wrote he said his section is called Piccadilly Circus!" She laughed a little. "But he said they need thousands more men because the enemy is very determined." Doris and I looked at each other. We admired Betty but we feared for her brother. We turned our attention to the road and a view of the Downs.

As term progressed sports and music clubs gathered momentum and I joined the choir to sing part of the Messiah. Rehearsals began for the Shakespeare production by the second-year students directed by Miss Hammonds. This year's play was to be "Hamlet" and Edith McManus was to play Hamlet. She and another student were to perform half each of the demanding part, Edith playing the death scenes because she was thought to be the more volatile actor. "A ripping idea," said everyone when it was announced. Finally, the cycling club was planning a ride to Bignor Roman Villa. When I wrote home my letters were full of the wonders of Sussex.

CHAPTER
THIRTY-FIVE

The Learner

One of the hardest parts of our training at Bishop Otter College was Teaching Practice. By the end of the first term we had begun to go out on single days to the surrounding schools to practise our skills. There were not enough schools in Chichester for everyone so some of us had to catch trains to nearby towns. I had to go to Havant where there was a big local authority school and I had to get used to the frequent travelling and waiting at stations. As it was wartime the trains were often late. I would check my proposed lessons sitting on the seat on the station platform. Often we went in pairs and the two of us would do our homework together on the seat. My earliest companion was a student called Peggy Foster and we quickly became friends. Peggy was plump and a joker. "There are two sorts of teacher," she announced, "those who have something to say and those who have to say something. Which are you?"

Victoria Road School was red-brick and newly built, with a spacious playground around it. There were four classrooms, each with about forty boys, who stayed in each class for two years, so that the children ranged from five to twelve years old. I was to work with the nine and ten year olds and Peggy with the infants. "Your form teacher is Mr Parker," the Headmaster explained to me, "and he will look after you." Mr Parker received me politely but without great enthusiasm. He had received students before. He had flat brown hair, a drooping brown moustache and a brown suit and he rarely smiled. He controlled the children with a stern eye. There were many boys from surrounding villages in the class and some of them looked very big. I watched as he moved effortlessly from subject to subject, first composition, then arithmetic and after a short break geography and nature-study. He invited me to help, but it was mostly by going from desk to desk correcting spelling or lines of figures. One day at last he invited me to teach. I was to tell the children about horse-chestnut trees. This was a subject I knew well and I showed the class the little "horse-shoe" mark, with its curve and dots at the joint, when you break off a leaf-stalk and which gives it its name. At first my voice issued in a hoarse croak as if from far away. But the boys listened politely under Mr Parker's eagle-eye and I began to feel more confident. They all understood conkers and I saw plenty more of them on strings in the play-ground at play time. The boys would chant:

Inter mitzy titzy too
Ira dira dominu
Out goes YOU!

as they struck their opponents' conker.

By the second term I could handle a whole lesson by myself with Mr Parker in the background. It was embarrassing to have him listening to my stumbling words and sometimes he had to come to my rescue — like the time when the story I was supposed to read to the class had fallen out of my folder in the train. But on the whole I was glad of his presence. I could see that some of the naughtiest boys would have been up to tricks without him. There was always the Headmaster's cane as a last resort but I had only once seen Mr Parker send a boy to be caned and that was because the culprit threw ink at another boy and spoilt his jacket. The beaten boy's mother was very angry and came to complain to the Headmaster. "I'll be up," she warned in a curt note. But when she heard what her son had done she strode home and boxed his ears!

Most of us students could manage the straightforward subjects like arithmetic, nature-study or spelling. The facts were clear and you dictated what the text books said. The difficult subjects were the less defined ones like handwork and physical education. A teacher was expected to be able to handle all these areas equally well. I was fortunate. I liked art and craft work. I was also good at music and could play the piano for the morning's hymns. (Mr Parker was tone-deaf so he actually found me an asset). But when it came to P.E. I was in trouble. We had to organise drill and special exercises designed for muscle-training. This was to be followed by team exercises with balls or hoops.

One day Mr Parker was away and I had to take the whole class by myself. The Headmaster offered to help but I thought I could manage alone. The morning passed fairly well but I could see the boys becoming restless and there was a good deal of noise. In the drawing lesson I allowed too much freedom and there were cat-calls and hoots from the back row and little pellets of paper landed on the floor while my back was turned. By the time it came to P.E. all was lost. The boys streamed into the playground and ran round and round imitating aeroplanes as I tried in vain to shout them into lines. When at last I gained some order for a ball game, one of the big rubber balls "accidentally" flew in the air and hit the window of the Headmaster's classroom. It did not break but a cheer went up from the crowd and the din roused the Head. He came striding into the playground and sent them all indoors. I was covered in shame and followed him inside as he rated the class. The ball-kicker owned up and was removed for a caning while the rest bent over their spelling books and there was no more sound that afternoon. But miserably I sat in the teacher's seat supervising them and miserably I went to see the Head after school. "That has put an end to my teaching career," I said to myself, and my tears welled up. I thought of my mother and how reproachful she would be when I returned home, failed, at the end of term.

"Don't worry," said the Headmaster kindly "that was bound to happen. You did very well all day, considering you were quite on your own. You need a little more practice and you will do very well. Mr Parker has given me a good report of your teaching." So I was not such a failure after all!

I flew for the train with relief. Peggy was waiting for me and I told her the whole story. Peggy had been in trouble with her supervisor. "She told me my writing on the blackboard looked like drunken spiders and that I couldn't spell potato," she said indignantly. We both chattered so much we nearly forgot to dismount at Chichester. All the students doing teaching-practice were having a stressful time we discovered. Worst of all was the appearance of the supervising tutor from College. The tutor sat at the side of the room and listened to your attempts with a critical look. She or he would then write notes and you knew you would be in for a serious talk when you arrived back at college in the evening. Some people were reduced to tears by the criticism but I was fortunate. Miss Hammonds herself came to my class several times, but always seemed to arrive when I was teaching something pleasant like English or History. She liked my choral ballad effort with Sir Patrick Spens and she approved my attempts to make the Armada a story dramatised rather than dull facts. In spite of her goodwill it was a strain to prepare so much work and to be watched daily in front of a restless class.

As a result of the strain, everyone became either very touchy or very silly by the end of a teaching-practice period, and the teaching sessions grew longer with each term. One such summer's evening we were in our dormitory preparing for bed. It was very hot weather and we were all wearing our flimsiest nightdresses. Betty Watson, whose long plaits were twisted round her head, had just taken down her hair, when a bat flew in at the window. It was very small and black and made a high-pitched squeaking sound. It flitted round and round the ceiling, every now and then flopping on to a bed or clinging to the door lintel. Everyone screamed and ran across the room. Wherever we ducked the bat seemed to be there. Betty, with her flowing hair, was in a direct line and the bat fluttered just behind her ear. She rushed for her hat and we all followed suit. "Open the other window, someone!" shouted Peggy, gripping her boater. "Ee, you won't get t'bat out that way, luv," called Mabel, who came from Yorkshire, "we'll have to chase it out!" Doris seized a tennis racket. Although she was tiny, she boldly climbed up on a chair and with great presence of mind biffed the skinny black wings. The frantic little creature circled wildly and then, as swiftly as it had fluttered in it fluttered out. We saw it dive behind the cedar tree and we sank onto our beds with gasps of relief. "Oh farewell ye virgins all," quoted Peggy, in mock sympathy with the bat.

Then someone started to laugh and someone else joined in. The joke was infectious and soon the whole room was in a roar. With nightdresses twisted round our knees and hats over our eyes we laughed and laughed till the tears ran down our cheeks and our nervous pent-up energy was spent.

Our first year was at an end. Exams were over. Hamlet had been successfully performed and the senior students were leaving. The war was building up and we heard ugly rumours of a big defeat in France. Thousands of our men had been killed or wounded as they retreated and there were urgent calls for more recruits. We were asked by the government to be careful not to waste any food so that there was enough for the troops. We were becoming very alarmed.

It was once again time for me to return to Somerset. It was a long journey and I knew I should not arrive home until very late. Fortunately the evenings were light. The experiment had begun called "British Summer Time" which gave the industrial workers and the Women's Land Army more working hours for the war effort. It was said that the cows would never recover from such violent change but when I got home my father told me they had hardly noticed it at all. Ethel said that at Batcombe Lodge they preferred the longer evenings. They could work in the fields until ten o'clock at night and it saved the oil lamps.

CHAPTER
THIRTY-SIX

The Demands of War

Life became grim. It was the summer of 1916 and I was at home. Affairs at Batcombe were in some disarray. Thirty of the village men had by now gone to the war and women workers were needed more than ever to replace them. There were heartfelt appeals for yet more fighting men posted at every street corner by desperate war ministries. Although over two million men had by now volunteered the German advance could not be stemmed and the *Daily Mail* told us that compulsory conscription would follow soon. Pressure was now put on those of our country who did not volunteer and they were made to feel guilty. In some places the "white feather" custom began. Anyone who seemed to be shirking his duty out of cowardice was handed the dreaded white emblem and made to feel a traitor to our country.

There was a cartoon in *Punch* which had pleased us at college. It depicted a young farm man milking a cow, being questioned by an indignant smart lady "Why are you not at the FRONT young man!" To which he replies "'Cos milk don't come out o' that end, ma'am!" In spite of attempts through humour, as the war grew longer the early euphoria had lost its momentum and more and more ways of persuasion had to be devised. Another poster in the Post Office read:

THREE TYPES OF MEN
Those who hear the call and obey
Those who delay
And — the Others
TO WHICH DO YOU BELONG?

Although farmers were producing twice as much foodstuffs, so much was going to the Front for men and for horses that people at home were running short. There were queues for bread and even more for tea and sugar at the village shops. Prices rocketed. Those with money could get food but the poor suffered. The *Daily Mail* now said that food might have to be rationed in the future, if people would not share.

At home my mother had a girl from the village to help her since I had departed. She was called Elsie Thatcher and she was a good worker. One day she brought in a letter. "It's from Bessie," said my mother, looking serious. "She says that Uncle Tom has decided to go to the war. He has signed on as a naval engineer. They are coming to say goodbye next Tuesday." Uncle Tom was younger than my father but still quite old for the Navy. He was the second person in our family to go to the war.

Earlier in the year I had heard that Leslie Pethick, Uncle Fred's son who had once teased us so jokingly over the guinea-pigs, was enlisting in London. He had been teaching languages at the Berlitz School and now he was leaving it for the Army. I had been up to London on the train from Chichester to say goodbye to him. He had bright blue eyes and was wonderfully handsome and I wondered why I had not visited him before, since he was my cousin. There was a new motor-vehicle called "The Tank", he told me, which was so huge and powerful it could roll over anything, over men and horses, over houses, even over trees! It needed engines to win the war it seemed. He said they would soon put the Germans to rout and he was very proud that he had been selected to be one of the first members of the Tank Corps. I had wished him well at his training camp and knew that by now he would be on his way to France.

Uncle Tom and Aunt Bess duly came and we all sat down for a farewell lunch. Everyone tried to be cheerful but I could see that Aunt Bess was unhappy. She had no children and would have to bear the parting alone. Uncle Tom promised to send Maurice a photograph of his ship and he gave us each half-a-crown. "Spend it on something you enjoy," he said jovially, "and forget this tiresome old war." It was with heavy hearts in the afternoon that we watched them disappear down the hill towards the station. We dared not express our true feelings and talked and joked but everyone had read about the German patrol-vessels in the Atlantic.

Autumn came and with it many changes. When I returned to college we were the seniors and it was our turn to look after newcomers. They seemed very young since we had grown into adults by now. We seniors felt it even more important to play our part as women teachers in the running of the struggling nation.

Universal education was at last being taken more seriously by the government and compulsory school-leaving age had been raised everywhere from 12 to 14, to improve the standard of learning.

Meanwhile the war was raging on. Interspersed with our good times were increasing days of unspeakable sadness when one or other of the students' fathers, brothers or fiancés was killed or wounded. They did their best to be brave, and we to be comforting, but in England all our confidence was faltering. The wounded were now beginning to return in their thousands from France and the big Graylingwell Mental hospital in Chichester had been turned into a field hospital as the loaded trains and trucks of wounded trundled in from the coastal ports. We began to dread the daily news.

In October I met Betty Watson with a letter in her hand. I knew before she spoke what it said, she looked so downcast. Her one dear brother had been killed in France. Her father had enclosed the letter from the Ministry. It read "Sir, it is my painful duty to inform you that a report has this day been received from the War Office notifying the death of Watson, R C, killed in action, October 1916." Betty went home to Washington for a week. When she came back she never mentioned her loss but she worked harder than ever. We felt awkward, and did not know what to say to her.

One day I received a hastily written letter from my Mother. It was to say that Maurice, having forged his age to 18, because he was so restless at home, had joined the Army. He and his friend Billy Pole from Honeycliffe Farm were on their way to France and his regiment had been deflected from Weymouth to Portsmouth. Would I be able to go and meet them to say goodbye? Ethel James would be there as well. I hurriedly caught a train and met Ethel at Portsmouth Station. Together we went to the crowded docks. After a short search there was Maurice, looking more confident and handsome than I had ever seen him, in his new uniform. He had a peaked hat and carried a rifle and a huge pack and so did Billy. It was strange to see the two Somerset boys so out of context but they were very pleased with themselves. There were hundreds of women saying goodbye to their men as the big troop-ships hovered above us. With a brave smile Maurice and Billy gave us both a last hug and Ethel and I said goodbye. Everyone looked so cheerful as they waved to the slowly departing ships with the brass bands playing. It was hard to believe that many might be going to their deaths with those triumphant notes. But as soon as they sailed out of sight everyone fell on each other's shoulders and wept and we wept too. The agonising thought of losing a loved one, now so nobly departing, was too much.

The following months were a nightmare for England. As the Germans advanced towards the Somme, men were being mown down in the trenches by their thousands. Night after night the troop trains came in to Chichester from France. Loaded motor waggons and horse vehicles brought the sick and wounded from the station to the hospital. From college at night we could hear their moaning and screaming as they rumbled past. The men were very brave but the carnage in France was said to be unbelievable. We heard about it chiefly from the families of the wounded when we seniors sometimes visited the hospital with gifts. It was not permitted for soldiers to write home in any detail about the fearful conditions at the front. Their letters were all censored so that they were only able to send home cheerful messages like: "The weather is a bit warmer", "I love you," and "see you soon, when we've finished 'em off." The tales of disaster from the wounded were very different and we could not understand why Lloyd George's government seemed so out of touch with the generals, so that they only gave us heroic messages about how well the war was going. We knew things were desperate.

A new horror followed. By 1917 the first of the German zeppelins had appeared over Britain, carrying bombs against which we were almost totally defenceless, our country as yet having no airforce of any power. The only hope for us in Britain was to shoot from the ground and in this respect the zeppelins were very vulnerable. One night as we watched from the window a zeppelin could be seen coming towards Chichester from the coast. It looked like a big silver cigar floating in the sky. Suddenly it burst into flames, as gunfire opened from the walls. To our dismay we saw figures falling out of it one by one. "Those are Germans!" cried a student. "They're still alive!" gasped another. "They won't be by the time they reach the ground," said her friend. We drew the curtains and returned to our studies shuddering. It was very horrifying and it became impossible to work that night.

Somehow we got used to the mixture of tragedy and heroism. Everyone knitted. If the spring of 1917 was

207

cold in England it must be colder still at the Front. We knitted scarves, we knitted socks, we knitted mittens and "balaclava" helmets and we knitted in our free time, on trains, on motor-buses (which were available now in Chichester) and in cafés. Women, children and even old men knitted for the boys at the Front or for the wounded in hospital. Someone saw a notice at Bognor saying "Wanted! Old bathing shoes to act as slippers for soldiers at the front!" and we started a comic collection in one of the college outhouses. There were even appeals for Easter Eggs "for our wounded Tommies" but we by-passed that as we would be away on our holidays.

It had been a terrible Christmas for the Hammonds family. Having survived the disastrous battle of the Somme the previous July their son had been killed in action while rescuing a friend from a blazing dug-out, just before Christmas. When we returned to college in January Miss Hammonds seemed almost her usual self but the Prebendary looked grey and worn and his wife was nowhere to be seen. Their son had won a medal for his bravery but that honour did not console the grieving family.

It did not seem possible that life could go on as usual in the college and yet it did. Lectures continued, students went out on school practise, we read essays to our tutors, people laughed and made friends or squabbled as usual. With the return of spring we cycled or walked on the South Downs at weekends. We loved to find the dew-ponds and the orchids which were special to the chalk downland. It was a popular expedition to visit the

Roman Bath House at Burton Park or Kipling's "Duncton Hill". We wanted to make the most of it.

On Sundays, having been to chapel in the morning, we were permitted to attend any church we liked in the evening, provided we wrote it down in the "Out" book. One Sunday two bold spirits in our year wrote "Greenfields Mission" as they sallied forth to the Park where officers could sometimes be seen. "They'll guess!" called Peggy after them. "They never look at the book," laughed the dare-devils. "What about your hats? You'll be recognised!" she continued, scandalised. "We'll look after them," they giggled and waved a large cotton bag that one of them carried. They were never caught and Peggy never told. They arrived back breathless in time for supper — with crimson cheeks. The tutor in charge gazed at them — and then walked on. She did not guess they had been talking to soldiers.

CHAPTER
THIRTY-SEVEN

Heavy Hearts

It had been a beautiful Easter with wild daffodils over the fields and violets and primroses bordering the streams. On Good Friday Frances and I attended the solemn three hour service in Batcombe Church. We were glad to be together again. Frances had not gone to college after all. Money had run out and the war had made things worse than ever for her family and for many other families, especially when a breadwinner had been lost. The story of the Passion had never had more meaning than on that Friday afternoon. On Easter Day a special prayer for the dead was read, written by Archbishop Randall Davidson, the Archbishop of Canterbury. Our rector, Mr Morant, encouraged the huge congregation that had gathered to be full of hope, in spite of so much terrible news.

"Christ is risen, Christ will come again!" — we chanted. It had upset my mother who was worried about Maurice. We had received only one letter since he left. It was full of cheer and made light of any hardships but it did not say where he was except that he was in France, so it was hard to know what was really happening to his Regiment. There was a cartoon in the Bairnsfather magazine depicting a soldier writing a letter home from a sodden trench under a hail of gunfire saying, "I hope this finds you in the pink as it leaves me at present." Maurice did better than that, but no news was bad news.

I returned to college for the final term. Summer was beginning and it was time to start applying for jobs even before we took our examinations. By the autumn of 1917 we would be qualified teachers with our own salaries if all went according to plan! I had decided I should like to start in Somerset, in spite of enjoying the beauties of Sussex, and I looked every week in the Educational papers. There was only one suitable job on offer in Somerset. It was at Wellington. *Wellington?* Where had I heard that name before? Then I remembered. It was the inspector who had come to our school years before and had told us about the Monument!! I had always intended to go there and here was an unexpected opportunity! I filled in the application form with some excitement and sent it off. Peggy, Doris and Betty had also applied for jobs in their home counties. Edith McManus, my sponsor of the year before, had already started work as a temporary war-nurse (and not yet as a teacher) in London. We heard that she was engaged to a young shipping clerk called Arthur Allison, but that he was serving with the forces in Palestine, against the Turks who had allied with Germany. I envied her speedy progress and initiative.

Our food, which had always been excellent at college, became plainer. We usually took plenty of sugar in our tea but the bowl was sometimes empty and we were forced to do without it. We heard that the German

submarines had sunk a great number of our foodships on
their way to Britain and we felt angry. Our bread was not
rationed but it was less plentiful. Neville Chamberlain,
the Home Front Minister, had asked us all to limit our
intake and the King himself was setting an example.
Cereals were to be kept for the forces, said Chamberlain,
and even farm horses were to do without them. The meat
which was so good for us was reduced from twice to
once per day and the usual Huntley and Palmers biscuits
were unobtainable. Notices appeared in Chichester
shops:

An Appeal in the Nation's Hour of Need
EAT LESS BREAD

We were glad to make these small sacrifices and we
repeated to each other in chorus the patriotic jingle from
a handbill that was prevalent:

Keep on Smiling
Don't look Glum
Half a Loaf
Is better than None

One day I was in the library, struggling with a poem
called "Sordello" by the new poet, Robert Browning. I
found the language abstruse but I sympathised with the
sentiments of Sordello, the protesting artist. Miss
Hammonds was very forward-looking in her teaching
and had also introduced us to another new, somewhat
outrageous, writer called Bernard Shaw, whose cynical

plays I read with great delight. I particularly enjoyed the predicaments of "Candida" which seemed to interpret some of our own feminine problems in a world controlled by men. Although my mother made all the rules in our house, I thought to myself, it was still men who governed the country and made our laws and waged war.

While I was pondering these insights a knot of students had gathered outside the library windows. One of them was holding a newspaper and they looked very shocked. "What has happened?" I asked anxiously as I joined them in the garden. "The Germans have sunk the *Lusitania*," they said. The *Lusitania* was a great passenger Cunard liner and it had been cruising round the Western coast of Ireland. There had been over a thousand people on board and they were all drowned. We were appalled. This was the ultimate German shame, we felt angrily, to have sunk a purely civilian ship with no defences. Wars were for armies and battle ships, not for this kind of cowardly act. What was happening to the world?

Our feelings of outrage were echoed by the nation. If this was what war meant then there must *never* be another once we had won this one. But would we win it? The terrifying unimaginable thought that we might lose had become a possibility in spite of all the propaganda and the patriotism. People no longer joked cheerfully about the "Germ-Huns", or about the "Conscientious Exhilarator" at the front, who cheered his mates in the dug-out. The war had become hateful and wasteful and everyone was exhausted.

The *Lusitania* was not the only endangered ship. Uncle Tom was in Naval Command and his vessel had been searching the North Sea for German vessels for many weeks. Aunt Bess had told my mother they expected a battle any day. She was right. When the battle came it was off Jutland and we only heard about it many weeks later. Uncle Tom's ship had received a direct hit and he had been in the engine room struggling to keep her on course. Uncle Tom was dead. It was almost impossible to believe. I began to understand the numbness and despair of the bereaved. I could think of nothing but Uncle Tom.

Life in college somehow continued steadily in spite of such terrible daily tragedies. We had student debates on subjects like "Women: Wives or Workers?" and "Can Europe Survive?". Among the first year students were two Belgian girls. They had quickly been dispatched to England by their parents as the Germans invaded Belgium and entered Ypres. They knew a lot more about Europe than we did. They told us that the Russian people were in revolt against the family of the Tzar and that a new leader called Lenin was rousing an all-out strike against authority to stop the pointless war. The Russians had suffered German attacks beyond all bearing. The two Belgians had peculiar Flemish accents and said "d" for "the", and "v" for "w" and rolled the letter "r". They were given the parts of Lion and Moonshine in "A Midsummer Night's Dream" and while Maria "beamed" silently on the lovers Anna produced a magnificent Flemish roar (both were ample-chested) and she even managed Lion's two lines:

214

You ladies may perr chaunce both quake and trremble
  herre
Ven Lion rrough in vildest rrage dod rroarr.

The Pyramis and Thisbe scene gained loud applause!
Few of the audience knew that the Belgian girls' parents
had been interned by the Germans and they had no news
of them at all, since the day they escaped to England.

Earlier in the term, to my surprise, I had received a
letter from the Front. It was from my cousin Leslie
thanking me warmly for coming to London to say
goodbye to him. He said he and his "tanks" were in fine
condition and he made a joke about the "luxury" dug-out
he slept in.

"We have a charcoal brazier," he wrote, "a bit smoky
but quite warm and I have just had a nice mug of hot
bovril and some bread. As it rained so much last week
our clothes are wet through and there has not been time
to change them as we are often on the move. So I have a
bit of fever. But we have plenty of cigarettes and tonight
somebody produced a copy of "Old Bill" cartoons and
we laughed like anything over each picture. Our — (he
meant "tanks", cut out by the censor) do not like the mud
so we are stuck here for a few days. But we have several
good canvas beds which we share in turns."

I wrote back immediately, trying to make my letter
both interesting and light-hearted. But he could never
have received my letter. He was killed in the first attack
at Cambrai. I heard from my mother that my uncle Fred
had received the news from the War Office together with
a posthumous medal for bravery. His only child, so

gifted and handsome, would never come home again. I never felt more sick at heart.

By now everyone knew a great deal more about the horrors our troops were undergoing. A series of poems appeared in a hospital magazine called *The Hydra*, written by soldiers. Two contributors stood out from the rest. They were Siegfried Sassoon of the Sussex Yeomanry and a younger officer called Wilfred Owen. They seemed to present a more vivid picture than anyone else of the actual circumstances on the battlefields. I read these lines by Owen, with painful sadness:

The poignant misery of dawn begins to grow . . .
We only know war lasts, rain soaks, and clouds sag
  stormy
 . . .Sudden successive flights of bullets streak the
  silence.

It was hard to know if we felt more proud or more disillusioned by the whole affair.

When we left the College in July we all felt we shared with Prebendary Hammonds some part of the bitter pain, with perhaps the glory, too, of family sacrifice which could never be healed.

CHAPTER
THIRTY-EIGHT

The Monument

I returned home by Paddington because I wanted to buy some special teaching materials in London. I was amazed how many motor vehicles thronged the streets, including trams. There were more motor vehicles than horse-drawn carriages by now, in 1917, many of them army trucks. Dozens of bicycles also threaded the streets, especially those with deliveries from tradesmen's shops. As we left Paddington I could see all the slum houses ranged along the railway. Dirty children and animals played in the gutters and women in shawls, some of them barefooted, gossiped at street corners or were queueing round costers' barrows. So that was London life! The war did not help matters in these city slums, with food so scarce and expensive.

The smoky train stopped at Reading and then at Newbury. I knew there was a large Internment Camp at Newbury where all the people had been put who were suspected of German sympathies. Some of them were totally patriotic but were merely unlucky enough to have German-type names. Our government did not discriminate. I strained my neck out of the window but Newbury looked very peaceful under the July sunshine and I saw no more than an old man leading a mule laden with stones.

When I reached home there was a letter summoning me to an interview at Courtland Road School in Wellington. I was in very good spirits because I had passed my examinations and received my Certificate at Bishop Otter College. I now felt ready for the next step and was looking for adventure. Frances was already earning in a nearby school, although unqualified, and we met at her house for tea. I did a gatevault over her gate for sheer exuberance and her mother clapped. We could forget the war for a while.

I had to change trains at Taunton to reach Wellington and when I looked out of the window I could see hills. "Those are the Blackdowns," explained one of my travelling-companions, "and look, in a minute you will see Wellington Monument." I strained my eyes. "There it is!" she cried, as a small grey point appeared on the distant horizon, looking just like the old picture. As we drew nearer I could see it really was in the shape of a sword and I wondered how far it would be to reach it from the town and if the walk would be difficult. "Take you about an hour to walk up there," said my informant, "and it's very, very steep until you get to the top. Nice place for a picnic though," she added, "and you can sit on top of the guns."

The interview at Courtland Road went well. There was the Headmaster, Mr Shepherd, and someone from the County Education Office in Taunton. Mr Shepherd though benign, seemed the old-fashioned type. What would he have made of our college education lectures I wondered? I answered various questions about teaching. "Miss Clacee, can you play the piano?" he asked, after a while. "Oh yes, I sometimes play the organ in our church as well," I told him. That seemed to clinch the matter. He needed a pianist. "I am happy to offer you the job, Miss Clacee" he said finally. My heart leapt. "Your salary will be £70 per year," said the man from County Hall, tilting back his chair, "and more the second year if you do well." £70 per year! All for me! I tried to imagine what it would be like to be so independent and affluent. I filled in a form, signed my name, and took my leave. As the Monument came into view again I called out silently, "I'll be back!"

When I reached home there was trouble and little attention was paid to my successes. A furious row had broken out between my mother and father. It seemed that he had made a complete muddle of his business deals and had got into debt. With the purchase of Batcombe Woods he had acquired various small properties and either through mismanagement or by failure of tenants to pay rents he had lost a lot of the money he could ill afford. "I shall be earning soon," I said, trying to improve matters. "Perhaps I could help? I shall be getting £70 per year." "Seventy pounds!" cried my mother, scornfully, "What rubbish! He needs £700 not £70!" I was nonplussed. I had no idea my father was so much in debt. So *that* was what all the rows had been about and why my mother was so angry and dominating at times.

Things seemed a little better after a while. Without Maurice, who always quarrelled with him, my troubled father seemed more settled. But because of the war he had very little help beyond two old men on the farm. He had given up the slaughter business which had been lucrative in the past and he now had only the farm and the future of that was in the balance. I had always hated the slaughter business because it upset me to see the animals going away day after day. The vans full of meat used, in the past, to come by our gate on their way to the station and I was thankful it had stopped.

I was glad to get away from all these troubles when the time came to go to Wellington. The little town looked refreshingly bright in the autumn sunshine with its wide main street and colourful shops and my spirits rose. I made my way to No 3 Hyacinth Terrace where I was to lodge, because the school did not provide accommodation. "Come in my dear," said a kind voice, when I rang the bell, and there was Mrs Hawker at the door with whom I was to spend the next years of my life.

Nell and Will Hawker were enthusiastic members of the Parish Church. They had no children so they took me to their hearts as their own daughter. I had all my meals with them and shared everything as if one of the family. Nell had brown eyes and a sweet face and was gentle and generous. She kept two little Pomeranian dogs for company, of which Will was rather jealous. Will was tall with a long nose and very garrulous. Having been brought up in extreme poverty as a child, he still tried to economise, for example, by walking on grass verges instead of asphalt to save shoe leather, or by undressing by the light of the street-lamp shining into the bedroom window, to save gas! But to me he was kind.

220

Will worked for Fox's, the big wool manufacturers who employed most of Wellington's labour force. While Nell knitted socks for the troops at home, Will turned out puttees in his department at work. Puttees were very long strips of cloth wound spirally to cover the leg from knee to ankle and they were worn by nearly all the soldiers at the front. They were khaki-coloured and kept their legs warm — provided they stayed in place. Some soldiers found them hampering while others used them as slings or bandages in desperate situations. Small Wellington boys could be seen any evening wheeling little carts, made of boxes on wheels, full of puttees for their mothers to stitch at home. They earned only a few pence but it was worth it for those who were poor and it helped the war effort.

Every morning Will and I set off through Black Path he to the factory and I to school. Wellington was a small town of about 5000 people. It had a small amount of industry but mainly it was rural. It was possible therefore to walk from end to end without difficulty, by footpaths, always with the distant Monument in view on the hills.

On my first day at school I was introduced to the other teachers by Mr Shepherd. There was a Miss Roe and a younger woman and a man called Mr Tucker. Mr Tucker was about forty. He had bright red hair turning grey, which he said to me, with a laugh, was the result of teaching ten and eleven year olds. My class was to be eight and nine year olds and Mr Shepherd said he would take me to meet them after prayers. Everyone seemed kind and helpful and soon we were in the extended classroom singing the first hymn of the term.

Before he took me into my classroom Mr Shepherd took me aside. "Miss Clacee," he began, "you may have had all kinds of new ideas given to you at college. Forget them all! We are a plain school and we want plain teaching. Do you understand?" "Yes, Mr Shepherd," I said, shocked by his attitude but meaning to work things out for myself. He then took me to meet the boys. There were 36 of them and they looked up expectantly. They did not look much different from the Sussex boys but they spoke differently. Although we all came from Somerset these southerners spoke another dialect from the northerners' speech which I was used to. Before I could teach them correct English I had to discover what they were saying because they wrote as they spoke. They seemed nice enough boys at first glance, but mischief would be hidden somewhere I knew, and my training days stood me in good stead now. I sat down and began the first lesson of my life. "Today we are going to learn about travel . . ."

Wellington did its share of war work. The Fox family, many of whom were Quakers, looked after a number of refugees from Europe. I looked out for Belgians when I met the refugees in the town. All the local men, except the sick and aged, had gone to the war and in the school we constantly heard of a father or an uncle lost and we did our best to be comforting. Things in Europe seemed worse than ever. For every British or French advance there seemed to be two retreats. It was rumoured that over fifty thousand men had been killed in one day during General Haig's great push towards the Somme the previous July and many people in England were on

222

the verge of despair. Were we really about to lose the war?

Around Christmas a new note of hope stirred every British heart. The Americans were coming! Instead of standing on the sidelines, the Americans had seen that a conquered Europe would not only be disastrous for Europe but a calamity for America too. They were coming to our assistance with thousands of fresh troops and bringing us new hope.

Just as we were rejoicing at this news and the Hawkers were reading out the headlines from the paper a letter came from my mother. She said they had received a note from the War Office to say that Maurice was reported missing, presumed dead. Billie Pole was also missing. Any further news would be dispatched in due course. I stared in disbelief towards the Monument.

THIRTY-NINE

Christmas 1917

It was the worst Christmas I have ever experienced. I returned home and I entered the house full of apprehension. Nobody said much. My mother showed me the letter from the Ministry but that was all. She remained tight-lipped throughout Christmas and my father escaped into the farm sheds where he busied himself with mending implements. Even that did not help because Maurice was the one who best understood how to do those things.

If only we knew what had happened to him! We alternated between hope and despair and as my mother would not discuss the matter I could only talk of it to Ethel James. "He might just be lost," she said. "He would not know his way in France if he was cut off from the rest of the gunners." (Maurice was with the Dorsets as a machine-gunner). If Maurice and Billie were dead it was tragic. Help might have been forthcoming, because now the Americans were advancing well into German lines.

I was too agitated to settle to anything so I walked down to the village. There was an eerie silence everywhere and I looked in vain for familiar faces.

Suddenly I saw a figure approaching. The person passed me without a word and went straight into the churchyard. It was Edward Fulford. Whatever can he want there? I wondered to myself as I looked over the gate. He was standing on the path, gazing at the tombstones. He looked even more strained than usual. "He must be the only young man left in Batcombe," I thought. "I suppose he is too full of nervous trouble to be accepted for the army." It was said he had a part-time job in Frome, mending clocks. It was also said he collected firearms and had a collection of antique guns and pistols. It sounded a strange hobby but we knew that in spite of his queer ways he had a good brain and understood mechanical things.

On the way through the village I met Mr Morant and told him I had seen Edward by the church. "Ah," said the rector, "he's going to have a lonely time one day. His parents are getting older. If this war ever comes to an end Mr and Mrs Fulford are going out to Canada to visit their sons, now that Mrs Fulford is out of hospital." "Wouldn't Edward be going with them?" I asked. "No, he would have to stay at home and be looked after by somebody." On the way home I met Edward again and this time he looked at me. His eyes were wild and haunted. "Hello Edward" I said, but he did not answer. By now he must be over twenty, I thought, and yet he still clings to his mother.

I went home troubled but I forgot about Edward when I entered the house. A Christmas hamper had arrived from a rich lady in the district. It was clearly meant as a gift of sympathy, as everyone knew about the loss of

Maurice and our predicament. My mother was furious. "We don't want charity here," she said fiercely and she hurled it into the scullery. We had no guests or feast at Christmas, just our usual roast beef instead of a goose and we did not even go to church. All the afternoon my mother sat staring at the paper while my father went back to the animals. Ethel James had her own Christmas family party, so I went up to my room and fell on my bed and wept.

It was a relief, once Christmas was over, to be back at school and I was beginning to know the boys in my class. There was a family called Sparks who all had flaming red hair and I had two of them. They fought perpetually but they never hurt each other. A boy called Tottle had tubercular knees and was in a wheelchair and I noticed the other boys were very kind at wheeling him round with them. Another boy who joined my class was called Frank Gillard. He had come with his parents from Devon. He was an unusual boy. He would sometimes come and talk to me at my desk in break-time and make all kinds of observations until I sent him out to play with the other boys. It was not long before Frank moved on with a scholarship to Wellington School, the big public school to which our brightest boys progressed. We did not guess then that he would one day become a famous BBC correspondent.

The only thing I could not teach was football and I left that to Mr Tucker. As most of the boys went home for mid-day dinner the staff had a break too and sometimes Mr Tucker walked part of the way home with me.

Towards Lent the weather grew warmer and everyone was gaining hope about the war. All along a fifty-mile front the Germans were being forced back and it put new life into our troops. We at home redoubled our efforts to save and go without. Although food was not rationed there were queues for bread, sugar and margarine in the shops. I read in the paper that a large parcel had been found dumped on the beach in Sussex, at Angmering-on-Sea, which contained pieces of bread and toast. This example of waste was held up as a national scandal by the newspapers.

"I expect someone was taking it home for his pigs and threw it away when he suddenly saw his lady-love," said Mr Tucker with a laugh.

I quite enjoyed our walks together along Black Path. I discovered that he lived in a hotel in the centre of the town called Shaplands. "They don't waste any food there," said Mr Tucker. "I sometimes mark the buns that I can't eat with my knife and I know when they come up again the next day and the day after!" He said he had broken his wrist some years before and it had not mended well enough for him to be accepted in the army. In any case teachers were "reserved", especially the older ones. I began to talk to him more freely and asked his advice on several teaching matters.

I also shared with him our fears about Maurice. There had been no more news from the War Office and still his body had not been found. Mr Tucker was very sympathetic. "It must make your teaching difficult for you," he said. "Tell me if I can help."

CHAPTER
FORTY

Turning Point

One day I went back to Hyacinth Terrace for lunch to find a letter waiting for me from my mother. It was not her usual day to write so I knew it must be important. I slit it with a trembling hand. What new disaster could this be? It was to say that Maurice had been found! She had written in a great hurry without details, but it seemed that a note had come to say he was safe and that he would be on his way home soon. There was so far no mention of Billie since the two, we knew, had become separated. I was so relieved and overjoyed I went straight back to the staff room and told everybody and they rejoiced with me. Mr Shepherd offered to let me go home, and Mr Tucker said he would take my class. But this was not necessary as it was nearly holiday time and, in any case, nobody knew when Maurice might arrive.

Soon another note arrived. Billie had been found! A group from the Dorsets had found him in a shell-hole lying badly wounded. They had picked him up and laid him on the horse waggon until it reached a hospital post. There, after a few weeks, he had been put on a train and sent back to England and "after only sixty five hours travelling" he had arrived at a military hospital in

Birmingham. There was much joy and relief at Honeycliffe and at the Beeches and now we awaited their arrival home with impatience.

When Maurice eventually came we were unprepared for the shock. He arrived at the station thin and gaunt and his clothes were in rags. He seemed quite pleased to see us, but his eyes were bleary, and he walked to and fro shaking aimlessly, and he could not eat the food my mother put before him. He hardly said a word to anyone but he smiled a little and then went back to walking to and fro. When it came to nightfall we tried to get him into bed but he would not go. He wandered out to the fields instead and lay down in a ditch. "He's gone mad!" said my mother, very worried, as they brought him slowly back into the kitchen. Next day she sent to Evercreech for the doctor. "He is shell-shocked," said the doctor. "You must let him recover gradually. Leave him alone and bit by bit he will improve. Keep him safe and warm." He soon had to attend a military hospital but he hated the restriction and they provisionally sent him home after a few weeks, to give him a rest.

The doctor was right, Maurice did recover. It was a very long time before he would sleep in a bed, my mother told me. He still went round the fields, lying in ditches, as though they were trenches. Months later we pieced his story together. It seemed that he and Billie had been in a battle of such horror that nearly everyone had been killed or wounded or got lost in the confusion. As the two ran blindly on together they had become cut off from the rest. Suddenly they had found themselves confronted by a young German in a tree. He was preparing to shoot and they had no option but to shoot him first. He looked them in the face wide-eyed and then fell to the ground, and they thrust him through with their bayonets. Was this murder or was it war? Sickened they ran on and somehow got lost in the rain and the fog and did not know where they were. Then they came across another division they did not know and got separated. Maurice soon left them and tried to find his own division, terrified he would be accused of desertion, and shot, but he could not find them. After that he wandered on through some swamps and and looked for food but could not find any. He did not really know what happened after that. Somehow he had reached a hospital post and after weeks in some crowded huts they had put him on a train for home. He thought he might have had pneumonia but he could not remember.

It was not until the summer that he became his usual self again. Billie was recovering from his wounds and they were welcomed back into the village. When in August I came home on holiday from Wellington, they were both on their feet once more and looking nearly normal. The awful question was, would they now have to go back to France? Although both were physically recovered the emotional scars of their recent experiences were so raw it hardly seemed possible. Yet the war was expected to continue for at least a year more and every fighter was needed. It was true that the British navy had made great headway in blockading the German ports while the Americans were keeping the Atlantic clear for our own supplies. Yet the fighting in Europe seemed more desperate than ever.

* * *

Suddenly everything changed. Wonderfully good news came through. General Haig had made a final decisive attack on the Somme. One month later our forces at last broke through the Hindenburg line. The German supreme commander asked to surrender! We knew then that the war was nearly over. Within a week the German government asked America's President Wilson to arrange a peace plan and on November 9th the Kaiser abdicated. The spirit of Germany was broken. War correspondents agreed that because we had harassed and deprived them of supplies so successfully by our activities at sea, the German nation was brought to its knees. On the eleventh hour of the eleventh day of the eleventh month of 1918 an armistice was signed.

The news spread quickly in Britain by rumour and by newspaper but there was still confusion. In Wellington we hardly knew what to do. The first thing people heard was guns firing and we were alarmed. Then the maroons hooted continuously which had usually been taken to mean an air-raid. But when all the church bells rang out as well we realised what it meant and everyone came out in the streets to cheer and dance. Soon in every window union jacks appeared and everyone stamped and clapped and men threw their caps in the air and jumped on the bonnets of cars. There was rejoicing in the streets all day and no-one could bear to go home while news kept coming through.

The following day everyone poured into the Parish church and there was a great service of thanksgiving.

Psalms and hymns of praise reverberated round the ancient Popham tomb at the end of the aisle and reached the rafters. Mr Pulman the vicar bid us remember the fallen as well as giving thanks for victory. I wondered how many people there, whose husbands or sons were gone, could truly sing, "Now thank we all our God." As the Last Post was sounded perhaps they felt, as Siegfried Sassoon put it later, that war was a loathsome tragedy rather than a triumphant victory. But for tonight, this one night, in sheer relief, mourning was put aside. There were fires at the Monument, fires on Samford Moor, fires on Blagdon Hill and on the Brendons and the Quantocks. Most of us went to Hilly Head where we had our local bonfire party. I saw Mr Tucker there with others and wondered who the women were. I wished I was in his group. We danced and sang round the fire and hugged each other, even among strangers, and food and drink appeared as if by magic. There was a pause in the celebrations and someone began to repeat Laurence Binyon's lines:

They shall not grow old,
as we that are left grow old.
Age shall not weary them, nor the years condemn.
At the going down of the sun and in the morning
We shall remember them.

Then we sang again and the festivities lasted all night long. There would never, never be a war like that again and we would see to it that there was peace for ever in the future.

CHAPTER
FORTY-ONE

The Aftermath

For many days to follow there were parties and processions, and the whole nation took a holiday. Lights blazed everywhere and church bells, silent for four years, rang out again. There was eating and drinking and some of it got rather wild. There were many tales of how the nation had celebrated the Armistice. A young boy in Trull had heard the news early from his father in Taunton and he had walked up and down his road with a home-made placard saying "PEACE IS DECLARED". He had tried to knock on neighbours' doors with the good news only to be sharply reprimanded by one, "Go away you naughty little boy and stop telling lies!". In London King George and Queen Mary had paraded through the streets in an open landau and soldiers had been raised skyhigh on peoples' shoulders.

At our school in Courtland Road we had a special Victory party the following week for all the boys. Many of them came in from the surrounding villages and walked many miles to school each day, so we had the party early to enable them to get home before dark. The women teachers and friends provided special sandwiches and cakes and Mr Shepherd led the celebrations, wearing a red white and blue rosette on his lapel. Mr Tucker did some conjuring tricks and led some games and every boy received a special souvenir coin stamped with the Kings head and the dates 1914-1918 on the back. We all wore red, white and blue paper-hats which fell off very easily. When mine fell off as I played the piano Mr Tucker picked it up and put it on my head for me.

Christmas 1918 was for many one of the most joyful anyone could remember and yet for many others it was the most painful. There were agonising gaps at party tables. We wondered at the courage of a neighbour being present at a Batcombe Whist Drive whose young husband had never come back. We celebrated, but at such a cost! By New Year the rejoicing had begun to get very out of hand as harsh reality emerged. There was so much drunkenness that some of the Public Houses had to close for a while for publicans to clean out their bars. In Batcombe, windows were broken and shops ransacked and as the policeman had gone to the war there was nobody to arrest the culprits. There were also a number of destitute men and women passing through the villages who seemed to have no homes or who were out of their minds or were looking for friends they had lost. Sexual immorality was widespread locally with husbands and fathers absent, and with displaced soldiers everywhere, and nobody protested.

Early in 1919 when the shouting had died down, everyone began to be aware of the terrible losses as men came back from Europe and the East. The troop trains rolled in to Taunton and gassed, blinded and maimed, men staggered home to Wellington and the surrounding villages. Many were helplessly shell-shocked. Over a million soldiers had been killed and over two million wounded. Our country had never known anything like it and we did not know how to recover.

In Wellington, those who could went to work in the big woolen-cloth factory, Fox's, already renowned for the puttees they made. The directors of Fox's had set up a junior school specifically for the children of their growing number of workers. This school was called Coram's Lane and it was considered superior to Courtland Road, where we taught. Its Headmaster, Mr Ebdon, was approaching retirement, and Mr Tucker told me that Fox's would need a new head as the school expanded. There was another manufacturing firm called Price Brothers at Bulford House, who took in more returning men (and women too) to make mattresses of a high quality. I sometimes saw Mr George Price, in his top hat, climbing into his horse and carriage outside the Squirrel Hotel on his way to the station. From there he would travel as far abroad as our colonies, selling the famous mattresses, and this meant employment for a good number of workers. But these workmen had been through four years of war — many of blazing hell — yet nobody seemed to want to hear their stories for long. The intense comradeship of the trenches, the wonderful heroism and the generosity of so many, seemed soon forgotten by the public. The saddest people of all were those too damaged to work again. They had to live on the very small war-pensions supplied by Lloyd George's hard-pressed coalition government. Their struggling wives queued for Rummage Sales in the Salvation Army Hall. I saw one of them carrying off my old coat and felt slightly ashamed. A stone war-memorial was set up in the Park with the names of all the fallen inscribed on it and Wellington people could meet there to say a silent prayer or lay a wreath. But there was scant memorial for those whose health was ruined.

Since they could not get any work some of them took to busking, which was strictly illegal. I heard that one day a penniless ne'er-do-well called Bill, from a nearby village, who had had a wooden leg since boyhood, attached himself to one of these groups in Taunton. But he could not play a musical instrument. So the buskers, thinking he was another ex-soldier, gave him the tin to hold before the passers-by. He collected a good deal of money. Suddenly a policeman appeared and everyone fled, including Bill, who was left with the tin. They never saw Bill again!

One day at the end of 1918 I was excited by an article in the *Telegraph*. Women had done heroic work in the war, not only in munitions factories and offices but as nurses at the front in the most dangerous places. Several Sunny Hill girls had been nurses and one of them had been wounded. The article said that Lord Asquith, who had so peremptorily dismissed the suffragettes and become famous for his "wait and see" policies, now promoted women's rights. Women over 30 were to be allowed to vote! The following year I went with Mrs Hawker to the Town Hall to register her right to vote. She was somewhat timorous because Will had been full of scorn. "If you let a whole lot of ignorant women vote," he pronounced, "it will undermine the constitution." But Mrs Hawker was quietly determined, so one day while he was at work we went together. I was only twenty-three so I could not expect such honours for a long time but I wrote to my mother and urged her to register.

It was some time after this that I received a terrible letter from Frances. Batcombe village had been devastated by an event which she proceeded to describe. The Fulfords had been preparing for their long-awaited voyage to Canada to visit their sons. They were leaving Edward at home but an aunt was coming to stay to look after him and Edward seemed content. Bags were packed and the day was drawing near. Nobody knew that, locked in his bedroom, Edward was trying out his firearms. One night, armed with a revolver, he had emerged from his room. He slipped along the passage to the room where his mother slept alone. Silently opening the door, and while she still slept, he shot her through the head. Then he put the revolver to his own head and blew himself to pieces. When they picked him up they found a note pinned to his sleeve. . It read: "I am taking her with me."

In the morning the whole village was stunned, bewildered, and silent as the grave into which they were both hurried. Frances said that instead of the usual gathering of mourners at the funeral, or the usual wake-feast, they had crept away to their homes and firmly closed the doors. She and her mother had done the same. It had been weeks before anyone could speak of the event at all and then only in whispers. Frances felt I ought to know what had happened and I was glad because I knew that my mother would never tell me. I remembered then the look in Edward's eyes when I had met him in the churchyard. I grieved for Batcombe and the Fulfords. The family had been our friends for over a generation.

There were many changes on the farm at home. Our milk which had been mainly used for cheese was now going into the towns to the new "milk-factories". With mechanical transport my father had only to fill his metal churns and put them at the farm gate for a lorry to pick them up on its daily round. This made his life easier as he grew older and as my father told me that Maurice was frequently absent "courting" in Wanstrow I was glad he had a regular market for his milk. My father also told me that some of the felled oaks were coppicing and showing signs of re-growth, but not the beeches. Beeches do not regenerate once they are cut down. Although the house was called The Beeches our lives from now on would have to take us beyond the beeches we had known so well.

CHAPTER
FORTY-TWO
Summer Sun

By now I felt quite at home in Wellington and I went to some of the Social Evenings and joined the library.

I no longer attended the Parish Church with Mr and Mrs Hawker. Instead I went to Rockwell Green, a village on the outskirts where the churchmanship was more in the style I was used to at Batcombe. The church with its spire was set high above the village. It had a good organist and I liked the Bach fugues he often played after services. One day, as I sat in my usual pew I saw Mr Tucker in the congregation. He usually went to the Parish Church so I did not know why he had appeared at Rockwell Green. When the service was over and I was walking back to Hyacinth Terrace he caught up with me. "May I accompany you home, Miss Clacee?" he asked. I was surprised but pleased and we walked back together. He dropped me at my house and said goodbye. Why did he come so far out of his way? I wondered. The next day at school he smiled at me as he passed through my room and a sudden bond seemed to have sprung up between us. For the first time we had met out of the context of school.

The next Sunday he was at Rockwell Green Church again! This time he was waiting at the door and we walked back together. He paused at our gate and we stayed talking for a while before he went on his way. We talked of Somerset and Devon and of how we both came from West Country farms. He said they had a fine church in their village at High Bickington and I told him about Batcombe Church built by the Glastonbury monks and how they had re-hung the bells in 1909 at the monstrous cost of £105!

Mr Tucker had trained at St Luke's College Exeter, beside the Cathedral which he admired, and I told him about Wells and Chichester. Then, "Do you enjoy the cinema, Miss Clacee?" he asked. I said I did, but we both agreed on the scorn with which we regarded the ludicrously romantic films reaching us from Hollywood. "All that 'Lovey-Dovey' stuff," he snorted contemptuously, "and nobody could ever live in the luxury they pretend is part of everyday life!" We prided ourselves on facing up to hardship and I agreed with him. Having shared such intimacies we seemed reluctant to part but eventually he left for his apartment at Shaplands and I went indoors warmed by his friendliness. To my surprise I began to hanker after an evening at the cinema. I warmed a fresh look at one of those romantic Hollywood scenes.

I found myself looking forward to schooldays more and more. Could it be that Mr Tucker was really interested in me, and was I right to be so glad to be seeing him every day? He was a great deal older than I, so was it a suitable friendship? I talked to Mrs Hawker about it. "Why don't you bring him in for a cup of tea if he brings you home from church again?" she suggested.

240

It was a good idea. I dressed carefully the next Sunday and went to church in good time. He was not there. Minutes ticked by and he still did not come. Was he not going to be there after all? The organ played and the choir processed in. He could not be coming now! Perhaps I had exaggerated his interest and he had merely been friendly. It was raining when we came out and I hurried home alone and shut the door of my room with a disappointed bang.

The next day at school he gave no indication of where he had been. I wondered if he had been visiting that Miss Bailey who was a teacher at Coram's Lane school and with whom I had seen him talking once or twice at socials. I felt agitated and began not to sleep well at night. "Never mind," said Mrs Hawker, "I expect he has a lot of engagements. He does all the hospital accounts and spends hours over those ledgers. I have heard too that he plays golf very well and I expect he gets invited out by friends."

The next Sunday he was not in church again! I began to feel absurdly annoyed and gave him quite a frosty look when he passed through my classroom next day. He did not even walk home with me at lunch-times. Either he was busy or else he went another way. By now I was ready to shrug my shoulders — as I thought. The following Sunday I went to Church quite late, thinking as I walked about a class expedition to Dunster Yarn Market which I was planning. He was there and already sitting in the back pew! All through the sermon I seemed to feel his gaze at the back of my head but I dared not turn round.

Unbelievably, the vicar's sermon theme, a quotation from Dryden, was "I strongly wish for what I faintly hope." I gazed at the floor and hoped nobody noticed my blushes. Was he speaking directly to me? I hastily pushed aside the absurd idea. We sang the last hymn and joining the throng I went out. He was waiting at the door and we walked back together. He said he had been away playing a lot of golf matches but would be delighted to stay and have tea with me today. "Come along in!" said the Hawkers kindly. Mrs Hawker fussed around her cups and her kettle and I brought down my books and photographs to show him. We bent over them together. As he left he invited me to a concert with him at the Town Hall the following week. Soon he became a regular guest at the Hawkers' house and we started to go for walks together round Hilly Head and Court Fields. He told me to call him Richard — or Dick as his friends knew him.

Dick smoked cigarettes, always through a tortoiseshell cigarette-holder, and he kept them in a silver case with his initials on it. I admired that and I admired his gold fob-watch which he kept in his waistcoat pocket. One day we walked all the way to the Monument. It was a warm spring day with scudding clouds. An ascending lark trilled overhead like a bubble rising in water. When we were in sight of the great Waterloo guns he suddenly stopped on a grassy path. "Norah," he said "I want to ask you something. I have been invited to become the Headmaster of Coram's Lane School and there is a house available with it. Will you come and be my wife?"

We were married in Batcombe Church on August 8th, the following year. Ethel was my bridesmaid and Frances was there with Evelyn, Mr Stenning came with his family, and Aunt Bess and Aunt Kit, and Maurice with Billy Pole and his family from Honeycliffe. My mother was smiling as she welcomed her guests to the house. It was a very hot day and everyone was cheerful as we gathered for our wedding-breakfast in the garden. My father in his best coat talked to the visitors from Devon and Mr Morant joked with his parishioners.

Suddenly there was a rumble and the skies darkened. "Thunder!" cried my mother "you must all come inside!" Everyone hurried in with table-cloths and dishes. There was a flash of lightning then the sky cracked and banged violently. The crashes continued, circling overhead, but at last they receded. There was a silence, then the rain descended. Presently Dick and I went forward to cut the cake. As we did so the skies cleared and a brilliant sun emerged. In and out, out and in, I thought. Perhaps that is what our life will be like. Perhaps that is what life is always like. We went out again into the garden.

Norah and her husband remained in Wellington, Somerset. They had three daughters. When the Second World War broke out, her husband stayed five extra years as Headmaster in the school which now bulged with London evacuees.

After the war they made enterprising expeditions to France and Switzerland. When her husband died Norah moved to Cornwall where the family had enjoyed many holidays. Later she lived in Farnham near a daughter. There she took up painting and sculpture, and several of her works were exhibited. She died in 1992.

Editor's acknowledgements

I want to thank the many people who have gone out of their way to give me encouragement and help of many kinds, especially Donald Sage, for continual support, Denise Moll, for the generous typing of several versions, and Elizabeth Dobson, for invaluable advice about publishing; Tony and Jill Clacee and Jane Ford who all provided transport and photographs and new information; Peter Collins and Tony Reid who made helpful comments on matters of natural history and farming a hundred years ago; John Allison, Caroline Bashford, Arthur Cotton, Derek Gill, Margaret Goodrich, Lionel Green, Chris Kohler, Joan Lampen, Hugh Mowat, John Voysey and Caroline White, for special information; Donald and Dickie Thompson and the staff of that part of University College, Chichester, formerly known as Bishop Otter College, for photographs; Nicholas Fisk and Hamish Hamilton for picture of old Lanchester car, and Hereford Records Office for picture of a turnpike gate. The Revd. John Hodder, Vicar of Postlebury, and the Revd. Anthony and Mrs Patricia Budgett, formerly of Bruton, the staff of Bruton School for Girls, Mr Joseph Tanner of Butler and Tanner, all of whom combined helpful comment with hospitality; all the other people, past and present, not mentioned above, who made this book possible; and, not least, my husband John, and our family, who have been forbearing and contributory during the extensive editing of this book.

I offer apologies if any material has inadvertently been used without proper acknowledgement.

Diana Hargreaves

245

ISIS publish a wide range of books in large print, from fiction to biography. A full list of titles is available free of charge from the address below. Alternatively, contact your local library for details of their collection of ISIS large print books.

Details of ISIS complete and unabridged audio books are also available.

Any suggestions for books you would like to see in large print or audio are always welcome.

7 Centremead
Osney Mead
Oxford OX2 0ES
(01865) 250333